Intensive English

Higher Intermediate Level
Students' Book

Meg Tafner
Tony Williams

MACMILLAN PUBLISHERS

First published 1988
Reprinted 1988, 1990, 1991, 1993

Published by MACMILLAN PUBLISHERS LTD
London and Basingstoke

Designed by Jordan and Jordan

Photographs by: Barnaby's Picture Library; Camera Press Ltd; J. Allan Cash; The Mansell Collection; Popper Foto; Studio AVP

Illustrations by: Rupert Besley; Joan Farmer Artists/David Bryant; Alan Gilham; Juliet Jefferey; Linden Artists/Malcolm Stokes; Brian Roll

Typeset by Katerprint Typesetting Services, Oxford

Printed in Hong Kong

British Library Cataloguing in Publication Data

Tafner, Meg
Intensive English: higher intermediate level.
1. English language—text-books for
foreign speakers
I. Title II. Williams, Tony
428.2'4 PE1128

ISBN 0–333–42089–6

CONTENTS

	Acknowledgements		v
	Introduction		1

House and Home

1	An Ideal Home	Uses of the Future: *will*; Present Continuous; *going to (do)*	2
2	Living Abroad	Reported speech: Changes in tense, pronoun, phrases	6
3	Man's Best Friend	Irregular past tenses and past participles, past habits	10
4	Operation Raleigh	Present Perfect with *for/since, just, still/yet*	14

Personal Relationships

5	The Perfect Partner?	Uses of Past Perfect: Past Perfect *vs* Past Simple	18
6	'For Better or Worse' – a Look at Marriage	Order of adjectives time phrases: *by/until*	22
7	Partner *vs* Partner . . . When Things Go Wrong	Modal verbs to express obligation and necessity; Phrasal verbs	26
8	How Good a Parent Could You Be?	Modal verbs to express suggestions and recommendations; Phrasal verbs	30

The World of Work

9	A Good Job with Prospects	Adverbs and sequences of adverbial phrases	34
10	Work: an Alternative View	Relative pronouns Vocabulary: headwords and definitions	38
11	Women at Work	Word-building with prefixes and suffixes Word order	42
12	Workforce 2000	Use of *it* as a preparatory subject; Prepositional verbs	46

Recreation

13	The Leisure Industry – the Brighton Bike Ride	Expressing preferences; Irregular verbs practice	50
14	Sport and the Tribal Instinct – Football Hooliganism	Conditional: Type 1	54
15	Lost and Distressed	Verbs taking the gerund; Sentence transformation	58
16	Where Sport Meets Politics	The Passive: Infinitive, Present Simple, Past Simple	62

The World About Us

17	It's a Man's World?	Present Simple for narrative and commentary	66
18	You Are What You Eat	The Passive: Present Perfect, Past Perfect	70
19	New Forms of Nuclear Threat	Conditional: Type 2	74
20	Famine – a Political Issue	Conditional: Type 3	78

ACKNOWLEDGEMENTS

The author and publishers wish to thank the following who have kindly given permission for the use of copyright material:

BBC Television, **Bob Geldof and Terry Wogan** for an extract from the listening transcript of Bob Geldof's interview on 'Wogan' (8 May 1986).

Council of Europe for an article **A Moment of History** by Benoit Heimermann (Forum (Issue No. 1, 1985)) (First published in Le Matin, August 1984).

The Daily Telegraph for the article **Boy, 14, wins divorce** by Ian Ball (Daily Telegraph dated 7 September 1985).

Christopher Jones for the words of the song **Back Home**.

Susie Long-Innes for the article **Successful end to Bahamas phase** (Operation Raleigh News, Vol III No 2 Spring 1985).

Newsweek for an adaptation of the article **The Decade of Women** by Marilyn Achiron et al (Newsweek dated 22 July 1985).

The Observer for the rewritten article **Caviar Francais** (Observer colour supplement dated 19 January 1986).

A D Peters & Co Ltd on behalf of the author and The Guardian for the cartoon by Posy Simmonds.

Times Newspapers Limited for the article **Computer Home on the Way** by Bill Johnstone (The Times dated 20 February 1986).

Transworld Feature Syndicate (UK) Ltd for extracts from the article **What changed the friendly face of football?** by David Block (TV Times dated 17–23 August 1985).

Every effort has been made to trace all the copyright holders but if any have been inadvertently overlooked the publishers will be pleased to make the necessary arrangement at the first opportunity.

The authors would like to acknowledge with gratitude the co-operation and encouragement afforded by Dr Norman Whitney, Paul Franks, Dilys Thorp, Glyn Hatherall, Shirley Asher, Nadia Taylor, Tony McMunn, Frazer McDonald, Ruki Shillam, Phil Older, Sarah Aspinall, Rob Franklin, Dennis Webb, Derek Strange and Kate Garratt.

Thanks are also due to teachers from the EFL Division, Ealing College of Higher Education, with students from the Council of Europe Summer Course 1986, who tested the materials.

INTRODUCTION

Intensive English is a topic-based short course for students at higher intermediate level. The course consists of a Students' Book, a Teacher's Book and a cassette of recorded materials which are an integral part of the programme of study.

The course sets out to provide the maximum opportunity for improving communicative competence. The units are designed to encourage discussion and role play, which present ample opportunity for individuals to express their views and exchange opinions in small group situations. The small groups in turn are often expected to make a contribution to a collective summing-up or comparison of results. The emphasis on spoken language skills is balanced by a variety of recorded pieces for listening practice, as well as tasks for written work and project assignments.

Project work can be organised on an individual or small-group basis and often involves some research, organisation of facts or data, perhaps the production of a report or visual display and finally a presentation to the class.

Intensive English is intended for young adult students. The topics chosen are slightly off-beat and have been selected to stimulate interest and provoke discussion in a variety of ways.

Each of the twenty units of the course gives opportunities for reading, vocabulary-building, listening (except Unit 10), discussion, role play, writing and additional project work. Each unit also contains a grammar section which analyses the language used in the topic materials and is designed to revise, reinforce or clarify the grammatical knowledge of the student within a context that is clear and comprehensible.

At the end of each unit is a 'Diary' section where students are expected to record and review work covered in the unit. It provides a checking facility based on self-assessment, and through it advice and further information or practice can be sought when a student feels that some aspect of his/her language or an area of the topic needs further attention. It also provides an interesting and valuable way for the teacher to check students' progress or problems.

Intensive English has been written to entertain, instruct, stimulate and generate a climate for discussion and the exchange of ideas, as well as to give opportunities for the important formal grammatical input that most students learning a foreign language need.

Unit 1

AN IDEAL HOME

There are as many plans for the ideal home as there are homedwellers. The first example considered in this Unit is the computerised home of the future; the second is an ecological house of the present – which failed!

Opening discussion

Explain the differences between these types of accommodation or buildings, then match the names with the pictures.

Working with a partner, choose one of these homes and plan the layout you would like if you had unlimited funds and could design the property from scratch. (Set yourselves a time limit of ten minutes.) Make your description as interesting as possible and present your plan to the rest of the class. They must then decide whether or not it would be possible or desirable to give you permission to build it.

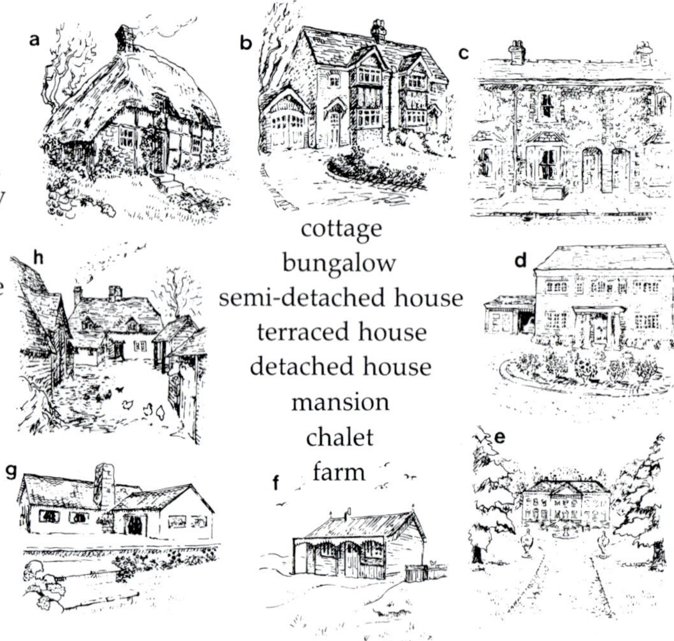

cottage
bungalow
semi-detached house
terraced house
detached house
mansion
chalet
farm

Reading

Before reading the text, check the meaning of these words.

commonplace
automation
consumer
facsimile
commuter
to link
consultancy
double
to monitor
consumption
to emulate

Computer home on the way

By Bill Johnstone, Technology Correspondent

Within the next decade computer controlled homes will be commonplace, allowing the average person to shop, bank and possibly even bet from the comfort of an armchair.

The boom in home automation is expected to be worth US$12,000 million a year in the developed world.

Details are outlined by Mackintosh International, the Luton-based consultancy, which has completed a five-nation study.

Advanced communications, information services and entertainment electronics make up the bulk of the equipment and services which will be in the automated home of tomorrow. The United States, Japan, Germany, France and Britain are expected to buy US$7,000 million worth of home automation equipment by the end of the decade. Five years later that figure is expected to almost double.

The home computer will play a vital part in the household of tomorrow. Through it will be channelled information allowing consumers to monitor and control almost every device in the home.

These units will be connected to a cable or small wire network installed in the home. Linked to the network will be a facsimile machine for receiving electronic mail, a telephone with an answerphone, a videophone (callers can see as well as hear each other) and meters monitoring the home's consumption of energy.

The computer will also offer to many commuters the prospect of working from home.

Work and home shopping and banking rely on homes being connected to sources of information. According to the Mackintosh survey, more than 600,000 Americans subscribe to an information service. That figure is expected to rise to 10 million within the next 10 years and to be emulated by the other developed nations.

Cable television is also expected to grow rapidly. That growth, matched by video recording, means that the automated home will become the prime location for family entertainment.

One of the first electronic shopping and banking networks has been set up in Milton Keynes, Buckinghamshire. The Midland Bank has linked 30 retailers to a computer control centre using electronic terminals, which allow shoppers to buy goods without using money.

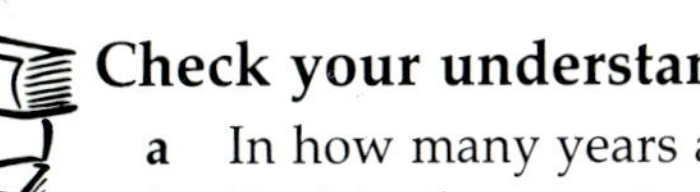

Check your understanding

- **a** In how many years are computer-controlled homes expected to be fairly usual?
- **b** Explain the meaning of 'boom' in paragraph 2.
- **c** What kind of function will the home computer have in the home of the future?
- **d** What does the term 'cable television' (line 62) mean, and how does it differ from the direct broadcast system?
- **e** According to the text, what has been achieved in Milton Keynes?

Work with a partner and present arguments for and against having this type of technology in the home. Make notes in support of each view.

Class activity

Organise a formal debate on the topic 'The home computer will play a vital role in the home of tomorrow'. Elect a chairperson and speakers for and against. Take a vote at the end of the debate.

Write a report of about 200 words for your local newspaper on the arguments and the outcome.

Listening

Now listen to an interview with Lisa Strangewater, a leading supporter of ecological living. Make notes under the headings below.

The location of her dream home	Plans for the house	Problems that had to be overcome
Cheshire	build solar panels	no sewage system

In the interview, a number of phrasal verbs have been used. Study the list below and listen to the tape again. Try to find another way to say them.

1. I didn't really *take to* city life.
2. We were *doing* the place *up*.
3. Rabbits were *coming back*.
4. We *got* architects *in on* it.
5. The ecology thing was just *getting going*.
6. It *let* the sunlight *through*.
7. It *gave off* methane gas.
8. My husband *ran off*.

1 GRAMMAR GUIDE

Uses of the future

The FUTURE SIMPLE is used to express assumptions about the future.

eg The home computer will play a vital part in the home of tomorrow.

- Look at the text and find three more examples.

The verbs most commonly used to introduce the future are:

think know believe hope expect suppose assume feel sure be afraid

eg I suppose they will come back late tonight.

- Make sentences using each verb to express an idea about the future.

There are other ways to talk about the future which we use more than *shall/will*.

The PRESENT SIMPLE is used to talk about a planned series of actions.

eg They leave London Heathrow at 6.30 and arrive in Paris an hour later.

- Plan an itinerary for your sales manager who needs to make a round the world trip lasting three weeks. His journey begins on Monday at 9.30 am from Gatwick Airport.

The PRESENT CONTINUOUS is used to talk about a definite future arrangement, usually involving a specific time.

eg I'm driving to Edinburgh tomorrow. They are following on by train next week.

- Talk about your immediate future, eg what you are doing tonight, tomorrow morning or next weekend.

The *going to* future is used to express some premeditated future intention or long-term plan.

eg They are going to travel around the world on bicycles.

- Talk about your long-term plans.

Practice

The left column shows what is wrong with an old house and an old car you have just bought. Make a list of all the faults. Opposite each, write down the improvements you intend to make. Now plan your weekend around the repairs programme.

eg The roof leaks. — I am going to repair the roof on Saturday morning.

The toilet is blocked. ______________________

The paintwork is peeling. ______________________

A window is broken. ______________________

The kitchen tap drips. ______________________

The bodywork is rusting. ______________________

Only one headlight is working. ______________________

The indicator is broken. ______________________

The tyres are bald. ______________________

The wheels need balancing. ______________________

- Question each other about your plans.

Vocabulary practice

1 Make the negatives of the following words using *un-*, *in-* or *im-*:

interesting	complete	economic
possible	appropriate	permissible
natural	popular	embarrassed
efficient	desirable	polite

2 Fill in the gaps in the following passage, using some of the words you have met in this unit.

My __________ home will be an ivy-covered __________ in the Cotswolds. It won't be __________ to look at; it will have low ceilings and thick oaken __________. It will be small, just two __________ and two __________ ; in the kitchen there will be an open __________ which will heat the house, together with the solar __________ on the thatched __________. But we won't need to do much in the way of burning fossil __________ because the triple __________ will keep the cold __________ and the methane __________ from the cess __________ can be burned as well. We will have to __________ the place __________, of course, and I won't mind __________ the water from the well.

DIARY pp. 2–5

Day(s) Date(s) Month Year

Texts

OK

Look at again

Ask the teacher

Look up in reference books

To remember

New Words

Grammar

Useful phrases

Unit 2

LIVING ABROAD

Have you ever lived in another country for any length of time? Read how one man living abroad had an embarrassing experience singing a folk song. Then listen to a song about a person looking forward to returning home after a spell working abroad.

Opening discussion

If you have ever lived abroad, form a discussion group with other people who have also lived abroad (Group A). If you haven't, form a group with others in the same position (Group B).

Group A: Make a list of problems you encountered while living in another country. Once your list is complete, arrange the problems in order, starting with the worst.
Group B: Make a list of problems that you would *expect* to meet if you were living abroad. Arrange your list in order, starting with the worst. Get together with a person from the other group and compare lists. Write a paragraph comparing your results.

Reading

Paul comes from the north of England. He spent several years living in Europe and, like most people living in a foreign country, had his fair share of difficulties. This is one of his painful memories:

'I lived in an expatriate community in Munich for ten years. Most of my friends were American but we had some British friends as well. At one time I got in with a group of people who were interested in Anglo-Irish and American folk songs. We used to get together and sing songs by Pete and Peggy Seeger, Ewan McColl, the Clancy Brothers, and Joan Baez, of course.

I had been playing the guitar ever since I was at school, but I knew I was not really a musician. I also knew that some people were turned off by my voice, which has a kind of nasal twang about it. Just right for English folk songs, but not everyone's cup of tea. All our American and English friends were very polite about it.

One winter my wife and I went skiing in the Austrian Tyrol. I took my guitar along to practise because I thought that would be a good form of après-ski for me. We stayed in a boarding house near Lienz. The proprietor was a very large Austrian. One evening he came over to our table and, in a friendly, threatening voice, told us that they were holding a concert for guests on Thursday evening, and that I was to play. I explained that I was not a performer and that it was out of the question. Never mind, he said, and for my sins I gave way.

On Thursday evening I strolled down to the room with my guitar only to find our fellow guests sitting in rows and waiting for the great performance. I did the best I could, and belted out a rather boisterous Irish folk song. After the second chorus I detected a glazed look coming over the audience's eyes and it dawned on me immediately that the last thing they wanted to hear was a song in English or any other foreign language.

I brought the whole thing to a rapid conclusion and crept off, to polite applause. One member of the audience came over to our table and asked rather timidly if he might borrow my guitar, 'By all means', I said, and he thereupon struck up a mighty chord, his neighbour hauled out a piano accordion and, as one, the boarding house guests linked arms, swayed from side to side and launched into a rousing chorus of *In München steht ein Hofbrauhaus*, the popular German drinking song. I paid up and hurriedly left.

Check your understanding

1 Explain the meaning of these words and phrases as they are used in the text:

expatriate (line 1) | turned off (line 7) | for my sins (line 18)
boisterous (line 21) | nasal twang (line 8) | belt out a song (line 21)
glazed look (line 22) | cup of tea (line 9) | it dawned on me (line 23)
hauled out (line 28)

2 What do you think the proprietor said in line 15?
   a I would really like you to play for us on Thursday evening.
   b You have this guitar, and you are going to play for us on Thursday evening, aren't you?
   c You are to play for us on Thursday evening.

3 What kind of a singer was Joan Baez described as? (line 5)

4 What is the difference between a folk song and a rock song?

5 What is the difference between a hotel and a boarding house?

6 Find an expression in paragraph 3 which means 'agreed'.

7 In the last paragraph, why does the writer use the expression 'crept off'?

8 Would you call yourself an expatriate? Why/why not?

Listening

Now listen to a song written by another expatriate.
The singer is Christopher Jones who wrote this while he was living in Beirut.
Before listening, read the text and try to guess what the missing words are.
Now listen and fill in the gaps with the right words.

Back Home

When I was back at home I used to have some fun
I used to go straight out when my ______ was done
And I never went to bed ______ twelve or one
And I didn't get up until ten . . .

And so tomorrow
I'm going to pack my ______
And ______ Saturday night
I'll be out of ______ place
And ______ a few days' time
You ought to see my ______
______ I'll be back home again.

Well I don't know ______ in ______ town
Because I ______ leave work until the sun ______ ______
And after nine ______ there's no one ______ around
So I'm always asleep by ten . . .

And so tomorrow, etc

During ______ ______ it's much too hot,
You can ______ die in the ______.
During the winter it ______ such a ______
That ______ are ______ in the street.
Yeah, I'm going home.
Well, as ______ as I'm home I'm going to ______ my ______
And ______ them to a party that'll ______ at ten,
And I'm never going to ______ away ______
After I ______ back home . . .

And so tomorrow, etc

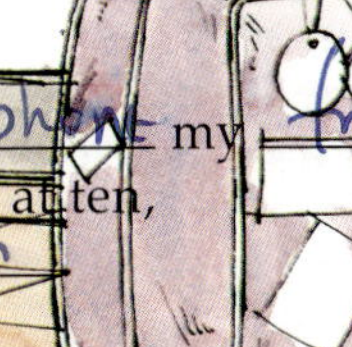

2 GRAMMAR GUIDE

Indirect or reported speech

To convert direct into indirect speech some changes are necessary:

1 TENSE — move into the past

present simple	⇒	past simple	will	⇒	would
present continuous	⇒	past continuous	shall	⇒	should
present perfect	⇒	past perfect	can	⇒	could
past simple	⇒	past perfect	may	⇒	might
past continuous	⇒	past perfect continuous	must	⇒	had to
past perfect	⇒	no change			

eg 'John has moved house', she said.

⇒ She {said / told us} (that) John had moved house.

Practice

1 Change these sentences from direct to indirect speech, following the example above.

- **a** 'Her work isn't as good as it was', Joe said.
- **b** 'They have been in the waiting room for ages', she said.
- **c** 'Martha will be leaving the house at six o'clock. She can put the spare key under the flower pot.'
- **d** 'Everyone went to the party. It was great fun.'

2 PERSON

PERSON	I	⇒	he/she
	my	⇒	his/her
	we	⇒	they
	our	⇒	their
	you	⇒	he, she, we, us, I, they
	your	⇒	his/her/their

eg 'I can't help you', Sue said to Richard.

⇒ Sue told Richard that she couldn't help him.

2 Rewrite these sentences in indirect speech, following the example above.

- **a** 'John, if you tell me what's needed, I can get it for you', Elisabeth said.
- **b** 'Our new house is wonderful! You must come and see us soon', Sarah said to Tom.
- **c** Eva told Christian, 'You can take my car if you promise to be back not later than nine o'clock.'
- **d** 'We think you should both go on holiday.'
- **e** 'I'm hoping that you can help me, Anna', Robert said.

3 ADJECTIVES AND ADVERBS

today	⇒	that day
yesterday	⇒	the day before
tomorrow	⇒	the next day
next week	⇒	the following week
last week	⇒	the week before/the previous week
a month ago	⇒	a month before
here	⇒	there or a specified place
now	⇒	then
this	⇒	that
these	⇒	those

eg 'I want to study this afternoon, then I can go out tomorrow night', he said.
⇒ He said he wanted to study that afternoon, then he could go out the following night.

3 Rewrite these sentences in indirect speech, following the example above.

- **a** 'I really want the work done today, not tomorrow', she said.
- **b** 'They left several months ago but they plan to be back next year.'
- **c** 'These books must be sent back tomorrow.'
- **d** 'There is a very good discothèque here. We can go either tonight or next Friday.'

Further practice

> When reporting statements or questions we often mention the *way* they were said or asked, or the *intention* behind them.

eg 'When you see Mrs Anderson, don't forget to thank her', she said to her son. (*remind*)
⇒ She reminded her son to thank Mrs Anderson.

Rewrite the following sentences in the same way, using the words in italics.

1. 'Why don't we go to the new Indian restaurant tonight', she said. (*suggest*)
2. 'You must come and have dinner with us', she said. (*insist*)
3. 'Would you like to join a group of us at the football match on Thursday?' he asked. (*invite*)
4. 'If you want tickets for next week's show you'd better book now', he said. (*warn*)
5. 'If I were you I'd go to the police immediately and tell them everything', she said. (*advise*)

Vocabulary practice

Choose the correct word from the brackets to fill the gaps in the following sentences.

- **a** If you do not come from an EEC country you have to register as an ________.
  (*foreigner stranger visitor alien*)
- **b** When you stay in a French hotel you have to ________ a *carte de séjour*.
  (*purchase complete obtain sell*)
- **c** Before leaving the plane, non-EEC citizens should fill in a yellow ________ card.
  (*emigration immigration migration ration*)
- **d** People living in Great Britain do not have to carry an ________.
  (*insurance card MOT certificate green card identity card*)

pp. 6–9

DIARY

Day(s) Date(s) Month Year

Texts

OK

Look at again

Ask the teacher

Look up in reference books

To remember

New Words

Grammar

Useful phrases

Unit 3

A MAN'S BEST FRIEND . . .

The English are renowed for being dog-lovers. The most popular domestic pets in Britain are dogs, cats and budgerigars or canaries. But we also have our share of the unusual . . .

Listening

Listen to Robert talking about his pet. Before you listen, read through the questions below. While you are listening write your answers in note form.

1. When was Robert able to buy his pet?
2. What advantages did his pet have over the usual domestic pets?
3. What is the popular misconception about snakes?
4. Name the type of snake Robert bought.
5. What does Robert mean by 'formal introductions' when he mentions his pet and his girlfriends?
6. How did the snake affect Robert's social life?
7. He says, 'They wouldn't cast a second glance at a T-bone steak.' What exactly does he mean?
8. What was the cause of the feeding problems?
9. Describe the alternative feeding arrangements and why he chose them.
10. What effect did the procuring of food for his pet have on Robert?

Group Work

Carry out a survey of people in the school and neighbourhood. Find out which pets they keep (if any). Bring the data back to the class and make a pie graph of the collective results. Here is an example of what it might look like.

Talk about the pie graph. Make observations such as:

The most popular pet in the area is . . .

Very few people own a snake and even fewer keep . . .

Most people seem to prefer . . .

Some people keep no pets because . . .

The most unusual pets are . . .

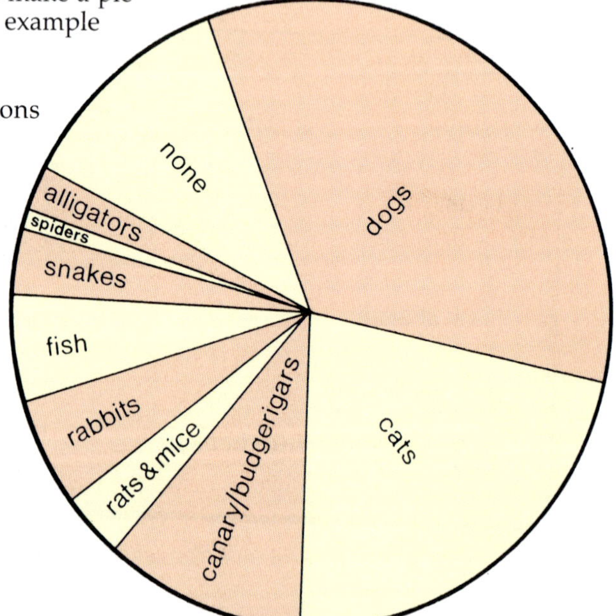

MAISIE'S AMAZING MENAGERIE

An ambulance and the RSPCA were both called to the home of Maisie MacDonald yesterday in the centre of Glasgow. A doctor visiting the house in answer to an emergency call discovered the most bizarre collection of animals who share the house with Maisie. While the ambulance was speeding to the local hospital with 83-year-old Maisie, a team of RSPCA vets and Edinburgh zoo-keepers were trying to solve the problem of who would look after Maisie's pets during her stay in hospital.

John McInnes, the Head Keeper at Edinburgh Zoo, had this to say: 'I have never seen so many different kinds of animals in anybody's home. I am staggered that anyone could look after so many creatures, especially at the age of 83! Maisie has done a wonderful job and none of the animals has been neglected in any way.'

Alan Marsh, 32, an assistant keeper, said, 'She has close to two dozen cats in there and four fairly big dogs, but they're not interested in fighting. It's unusual to find such placid animals as these. They live mainly on the ground floor. The rest of the house is huge. There seems to be something different in every room.'

RSPCA Inspector, Bill Miles, told our reporter, 'We are making every effort to keep Maisie's pets alive and well until she is released from hospital. I think we will have to consider the possibility of fostering many of them with families around Glasgow! The others can be taken to the zoo.'

So what exactly did they find in Maisie's house? There were cages of birds of all shapes and colour going up the three flights of stairs. A goat and several families of rabbits shared a room on the first floor. The bathroom had been taken over by a pair of mallard ducks and a Canada goose, a giant fish tank in another bedroom housed a collection of terrapins and salamanders. Yet another fish tank held a pair of baby alligators! But the top floor was the most surprising of all. A fully grown tiger was living in the attic! However, the zoo-keepers reported that it was as tame as a kitten and they had no trouble persuading it to get into the van to go to the zoo.

From her hospital bed Maisie, suffering from a fractured hip, said, 'My animals are my whole life. I was cleaning out Rajah the tiger's room this morning when he got too playful and knocked me down. I managed to drag myself out and called one of the dogs. I often send him to the Post Office with a note to get things for me, so this time I sent him with a note asking for help. Everyone has been so kind, but I'm terribly worried about my pets.'

Vocabulary check

Find words or phrases in the text which mean the same as the following:

1 astonished
2 strange
3 non-aggressive
4 trying hard
5 contained
6 gentle
7 broken
8 concerned

Activity

Working in pairs or small groups, prepare the script for a television appeal to families in the area to look after Maisie's pets until she is able to come out of hospital. Choose one person from each group to 'broadcast' the appeal. The class must then decide whose appeal would be the most effective.

Past simple of irregular verbs

Complete the sentences using the past simple or past participle forms of the verbs in brackets.

At one time Robert (breed) snakes in his garden shed. At first he (feed) them mice and rats but he (find) that rather difficult in the long run. The neighbours complained, but he (fight) to continue his hobby. They (think) that he was stealing their pets to feed the snakes.

Robert (go) into the garden and (dig) a hole. He put his hand into a bag, (take) out an object and (fling) it into the hole. The neighbours (understand) that he was up to no good. While they were watching, he (stride) off back into the house.

Past continuous

The Past Continuous is used with an adverb to link continuous activities in the past.

eg While the ambulance was speeding to the local hospital, a team of RSPCA vets and Edinburgh Zoo keepers were trying to solve the problem of who would look after Maisie's pets.

Practice

Join pairs of sentences from the list below to make sensible statements, using *just as/ while/ when*.

they were watching a horror film	I was studying for exams
he was cleaning the car	you were waiting outside the cinema
she was calling the police	we were trying to get through the traffic jam

Past simple/ past continuous

Explain the difference in meaning between the following sentences.

When Richard arrived she was making tea.

When Richard arrived she made tea.

Write down five similar examples of your own. Ask your partner to explain the difference.

Past habits

Would + infinitive is used to talk about habitual actions in the past.

eg 'Off I would go and there would be a dear old lady fussing over her cat.'

Think of five things that you habitually did during your early days at school. Write them down, using *would*.

Practice

Now look at the passage below and decide whether the correct form of the verbs in brackets should be Past Simple or *would* + infinitive.

My grandfather always (get) up at half past five. He (work) in the local brick works which (be) two miles away. He (leave) the house at six and (walk) to work whatever the weather. His lunch (always be) the same – freshly-baked bread, cheese and some fruit. He (always eat) with the workers even though he (be) the manager.

Vocabulary practice

All the animals below have been mentioned in this Unit. Try to place each animal in the appropriate cage. All animals of the same type should go together. But what do we mean by 'type'? The only clue is the word at the top of each cage. When you have finished, give your reasons for grouping the animals as you have. (If your answers are correct, each animal should appear in one cage only.)

dog budgerigar cat snake rabbit duck goose rat terrapin alligator salamander tiger kitten boa constrictor mouse fish gerbil

dog	goose	rat	salamander

Writing

Your local council is trying to close down the animal clinic in your area. There isn't another one in a nearby town.

Look at your survey of pet owners again, and write a report to the local council making recommendations to either support or oppose the closure of the clinic. Use any data from your survey that may be relevant and add your own comments and observations.

Work in small groups or pairs. The report should be no more than 500 words.

DIARY

pp. 10–13

Day(s) Date(s) Month Year

Texts

OK

Look at again

Ask the teacher

Look up in reference books

To remember

New Words

Grammar

Useful phrases

Unit 4

OPERATION RALEIGH

Operation Raleigh is a scheme for sending young people on a voyage around the world during which they have to carry out projects to help communities with urgent needs.

Listening 1:

Lucy spent three months of 1985 working as a venturer with Operation Raleigh. Listen to Lucy's account of the background to the scheme and then complete the sentences below.

1 During 1978 to 1980, the explorer Colonel John Blashford-Snell and a team of experts ________________.

2 This series of events was known as ________________.

3 It was designed to provide ________________.

4 Those taking part were aged between ________________.

5 Before the operation was completed, Prince Charles suggested ________________.

6 Operation Raleigh is to involve over ________________
for a period of ________________.

7 The venturers will be selected from ________________.

8 Each venturer is expected to ________________.

Group discussion

Each prospective venturer selected for Operation Raleigh must raise about £1500. In your groups, draw up a list of plans for raising that amount of money for each person within six weeks. Present your ideas to the class. Take a vote on which plans would be the most successful.

Listening 2:

Lucy is now talking about her personal experiences as a venturer on Operation Raleigh. Make notes under these headings:

The project	Hardships	Local community	Benefits: community & personal

Compare your notes with a partner. Make a list of new words and use a dictionary to find out their meanings. You will need all this information later.

Writing

Using information gathered from Listening parts 1 and 2, and any data from the text, write a news article of not more than 500 words on Operation Raleigh for your local or community newspaper. Think of a suitable headline and plan any illustrations you need.

Successful end to Bahamas phase

Susie Long-Innes, Press Officer on SES Sir Walter Raleigh

The first phase of Operation Raleigh drew to a close in Freeport, Grand Bahama on March 6. The group of international Venturers could look back on their past 3 months' work with pride and a sense of achievement. Most of the planned projects were completed, together with a great many more which arose along the way.

Wherever the name Operation Raleigh has been mentioned, it has been greeted with interest and enthusiasm. Local people have sponsored us with all kinds of food and equipment, but maybe more importantly, we have been shown kindness and generous hospitality at every point.

Not only have the Venturers learned how to communicate with each other within the group, but they have also learned how rewarding it is to put something into a community. They have helped with conservation projects trying to preserve the local conch and fish life, they have seen the pleasure on the faces of children at the completion of a basketball pitch on North Caicos, and they have watched the children from the children's home on Grand Bahama swarming over each piece of equipment at the adventure playground as it was erected.

Local Bahamian people have been involved with all the projects in one way or another. The expedition to Cat Island was dependent on the local community for directions to clean water wells; Bart from the Cutlass Bay Club will be remembered for his never-ending kindness and advice to the expedition, and a quick lesson in the art of making guava bread proved a cheap and popular way of satisfying hungry Venturers. The newly opened Lucayan National Park with its mile of pathways and unique caverns system is a monument to the Venturers who worked on it, and a potential dollar-spinner for Freeport's tourist industry.

Visits and lectures to schools have been a feature of most of the expeditions, and wherever possible the children have been able to visit the Flagship. On one memorable occasion in Freeport, Captain Mike Kichenside was spotted disappearing down a hatch leading into the engine room, chasing one particularly evasive youngster, while over 1000 of the boy's school mates rampaged over the ship, the Acorn computer room proving to be an irresistible magnet.

Some Venturers arrived on the expedition armed with specialist skills, but most went home well prepared to cope with varied situations. An aircraft instruments engineer, Nick Brookes, found himself faced with the task of preparing Christmas Day breakfast for 200, while Simon Frame from Wales reckons he has cooked corned beef in more than a dozen ways, with fried potatoes skins mixed with Burgess relish voted as the most popular side-dish!

Resourcefulness has also proved the key to the living accommodation.

Venturers built 'bivvies' from plastic sheets, plywood or palm fronds – one even used the J&B sail. Basic skills in carpentry, rope work and boathandling have been learnt by most, whilst those involved with Reefwatch and the Seagrass projects have learnt how to judge distance and depth underwater to within a few feet.

Vocabulary practice

1 Find words or phrases in the text with the same (or similar) meaning as these:

lines 5–41
- **a** ended
- **b** review
- **c** assisted
- **d** satisfying
- **e** built

lines 42–79
- **f** somehow
- **g** money-maker
- **h** unforgettable
- **i** seen
- **j** ran about

lines 80–110
- **k** attraction
- **l** confronted by
- **m** thinks
- **n** shelters
- **o** estimate

GRAMMAR GUIDE

Present Perfect

With *for* and *since*

Present Perfect + *for* refers to a period of time extending into the present. It is used with a number of days, weeks, etc.

eg We have lived here for years.

Present Perfect + *since* is used with a specific time and means from that time to the present.

eg They have had that car since February.

Practice

1 Put the time phrases below into the correct boxes under *for* or *since*, then make sentences using two examples from each box.

FOR		SINCE
	Christmas last week five minutes your birthday six years half a century last August a fortnight some time he left school	

2 Rewrite these sentences using the present perfect with either *for* or *since*, as in the example.
eg John went to Glasgow in 1978. He is still living there. (*since*)
⇒ John has been living in Glasgow since 1978.

- **a** It is 7.30 am. Anna is waiting for the bus. She went to the bus stop an hour ago. (*since*)
- **b** Grandmother came to stay on Christmas Eve and she hasn't gone home yet. (*since*)
- **c** He started playing tennis when he was 18. He is now 57 and he still plays regularly. (*for*)
- **d** She started writing a novel two years ago. It isn't finished yet (*since*)
- **e** My parents emigrated to Australia in 1970. They are still living there. (*for*)

With *just/still/yet*

Present Perfect + *just* is used for recently completed action.

eg They have just arrived from New York.

Present Perfect + *still* is used with a negative verb to denote something that has not happened but is expected. *Still* always follows the subject of the verb.

eg He still hasn't paid the rent.

Present Perfect + *yet* + negative verb also indicates that something is expected in the future and has not happened. *Yet* normally appears at the end of the sentence.

eg I've been here for an hour and she hasn't arrived yet.

Practice

Make sentences with the following words, using *for/since/still/yet*. There may be more than one correct answer.

eg I/not eat/lamb/Easter

⇒ I haven't eaten lamb since Easter.

1 They/study/English/French/ six months
2 She/write/book/1982
3 We/decorate/house/every weekend/not finish
4 He/not sit/exam
5 He/try/few times/but/not pass/driving test

Vocabulary practice

Choose the correct word in italics to fill the gaps in each of these sentences.

1 Many youngsters like camping because it appeals to their spirit of ________
(*adventure venture advent event*)
2 When sailing in shallow waters you have to learn how to ________ depth underwater.
(*adjudge measure judge see*)
3 At night it is possible to ________ your position by looking at the stars.
(*lose see navigate estimate*)
4 Many countries have sent exploration ________ to the Antarctic.
(*exhibitions expositions tours expeditions*)
5 Instructors teach children the art of ________ in the desert or at sea.
(*survival drinking navigation fishing*)
6 The best leaders are those who show ________ when things go wrong.
(*cleanliness cleverness resourcefulness artfulness*)
7 At the end of the holiday the children struck ________ and put their tents into the van.
(*camp tentpegs out lucky*)
8 If you have no tents you can make ________ out of tree branches.
(*beverages bivouacs kerouacs huts*)
9 This training gives youngsters the ability to ________ with varied situations.
(*hope cope manage handle*)
10 Most sailors ought to be able to build a ________ bridge.
(*iron transporter swing rope*)

DIARY pp. 14–17

Day(s) Date(s) Month Year

Texts

OK

Look at again

Ask the teacher

Look up in reference books

To remember

New Words

Grammar

Useful phrases

Unit 5

THE PERFECT PARTNER?

Choosing the right partner is not, and has never been, easy. A young woman from Trinidad chose an unusual method of finding her life mate, who was a convicted murderer.

Group discussion

If you were looking for someone to love and possibly marry, which of these do you think would be the best way to find the right person? Record the views of your group in note form, then compare them with those of the other groups.

a Try computer dating.

f Advertise in the personal columns of local newspapers.

b Let your parents choose for you.

e Wait until someone falls in love with you.

c Wait until you fall in love.

Choose from this list the qualities you would look for in your perfect partner and add any others you can think of. Arrange your list in order of priority and do a survey of the class to find out if their priorities were the same as yours.

vivacious	good dancer
tall	good-looking
vegetarian	serious
wealthy	romantic
witty	sense of humour

d Consult an astrologer.

Listening

Computer dating agencies are generating a great deal of money for the people who run them, but do they also generate a similar number of satisfied customers? Is it really possible to find the person of your dreams when a machine carries out the selection on your behalf?

Listen to the telephone conversation on the tape, make notes and answer the questions.

Find reasons why

1 the caller is making enquiries;
2 the dating agency exists;
3 the members are not screened;
4 the fees are high.

Find out what

5 the membership fees are:
6 a member is given on payment of fees;
7 the total membership is;
8 kind of people join the agency;
9 the caller decides to do.

Reading

How to Marry a Murderer

Virginia Harris was sitting at home in Battersea, London, watching TV, when she first caught sight of the man who was to be her husband. The moment she saw his face and eyes as he looked out at her from the television screen, her heart went out to him. Whatever she did she couldn't forget him.

The only trouble was, the man she had fallen in love with was serving a life sentence for murder in San Quentin prison, San Francisco. At one time he had been waiting his turn for the gas chamber. He had a long criminal record behind him and had found his way into Death Row after a bloody gun battle with the police in which he had killed two people and injured two others. The sentence had afterwards been commuted to life imprisonment.

Virginia did not want her perfect partner to be a murderer but the power of love – even at this distance – overcame all obstacles, and eventually Virginia found her way to her intended in prison and married him. Even now she does not know what drew her to Hasan Brown and why she should want to marry a murderer. She is an attractive and intelligent woman, and perhaps she felt that she could lead him back to the straight and narrow. Or perhaps she was lonely and desperate and was prepared to overlook even violent crime in the hope of finding love. 'When I saw him on television I just felt this need to get in touch with him, I didn't know why.'

The initial problem was establishing contact. After deciding to write to him, and finding his exact address, her main concern was to pick the right words. She didn't want to appear as a crank or a do-gooder, so she simply told him about her life. She told him that she had come to England as a young child from Trinidad, that she was 36 years old, was divorced and had three children, the eldest aged nineteen. She told him that she liked reggae music and had met Stevie Wonder and Marvin Gaye.

Hasan, the murderer, could not believe his good fortune. 'I looked upon her writing as a gift from God. From halfway round the world a female finds me. Is that not a gift?' So he wrote back. The correspondence grew from one letter every ten days to once a day. Eventually it became more serious. 'Hasan told me that from my very first letter he knew that he wanted me to be his wife because he felt that we communicated very well . . . and I began to look at him in a completely different light.'

Hasan wrote that marriages in prison were not out of the question and there was even a room set aside for marriage ceremonies and a caravan parked in a compound where they could spend their honeymoon. Finally she achieved her dream, and a TV company flew out with her to film the ceremony. Virginia was crying tears of joy as she ran down the corridor of the prison into the arms of the man she loved, and hugged him. After a few days they married.

After their caravan-park honeymoon ended, the harsh reality began. Hasan returned to his cell and she flew back to England to try to resume a normal life. The letters continue, but now her last phone bill came to £400. She wants to move out to California with her children in order to be near her husband and visit him more often. But she has great financial problems. She hopes that he will be out in one year – she believes that Hasan killed only one man and that was in self-defence, and this is what she tells her children – but the prison authorities, looking at his long criminal record, say it is more likely to be ten.

The prison authorities are also sceptical about women who marry prisoners: 'A lot of it is due to a sense of romance', said one officer, 'It's very romantic in some women's eyes to have a prisoner for a husband or boyfriend. They like the thrill of being married to someone who's lived on a razor's edge.

'On a lot of occasions the inmate discards the woman as soon as he gets out. With her help he proves to the Prison Release Board that he's going to be a stable individual. But afterwards he doesn't need her any more.'

But, as Virginia said, 'My eldest son said to me that I should do what is going to make me happy, so I really don't care what anyone else thinks.'

Vocabulary check

1 Find two phrases in paragraph 1 which can mean 'attracted to'.
2 Find three words in the passage which refer to prison facilities or accommodation.
3 Identify a word in paragraph 2 which means 'changed'.
4 Which phrase in paragraph 3 means 'an honest life'?
5 Explain 'someone who's lived on a razor's edge' in paragraph 8.

Check your understanding

1 Are there any clues in the text to indicate how Virginia managed to finance her trip to California?
2 Is there anything in the text to suggest that Virginia is indulging in wishful thinking?
3 Hasan was of the opinion that the interest taken in him by Virginia was a divine gift. Can you find anything in the text to support that idea?

Writing

Look at the reading text again. Check each paragraph and make a note of the main point or points. When you have done this, using only your notes, write a short summary of the passage (200 words maximum).

Past Perfect

> The Past Perfect can be the past equivalent of the Present Perfect tense (action extends to *now*). In Past Perfect clauses, the action extended to *then* and the point of time which defines *then* is either mentioned or implied.

eg The football match has started.
⇒ The football match had started by the time he arrived.

> Past Perfect + *since/for/always/never/just* etc, can be used for an action which began in the past before the time of speaking and went up to that time or just before it.

eg He has been a missionary for twelve years. He loves the life.
⇒ When I met him he had been a missionary for twelve years and loved the life.

> The Past Perfect can also be the past equivalent of the Past Simple. It is used when we look back on an earlier action.

eg I had just got into the bath when the phone rang.
(**Note**: an ordinary sequence of past events needs no perfect tense when there is no looking back.)

> The Past Perfect is used after *when* to emphasise that the first action happened before the second began.

eg When he had had ten hours of driving instruction he was ready to take the test.

> Time clauses introduced by *when/until/as soon as/before/after* are normally used with a perfect tense

eg After they had disconnected the burglar alarm they went silently into the house through the window.

Practice

Put the verbs in brackets into the Past Simple or Past Perfect.

1. He (realise) he (forget) his key after he (shut) the door.
2. Someone (steal) his motorcycle just after he (buy) it.
3. The Fire Brigade (arrive) when the house (burn down).
4. As soon as they (get) home, Joanna (feel) quite ill.
5. It wasn't until she (taste) the casserole that she (know) it (be) a complete disaster.
6. They just (begin) to enjoy the drive when one of the tyres (burst).
7. The builders (start) the alterations to the house as soon as the materials (arrive).
8. Someone (crash) into our car before we (had) it for two months.
9. They (find) out about the changes the company (plan) to make long before the official announcement (appear) in the press.
10. Just after she (left) the supermarket she (realise) she (leave) her cheque book behind.

Vocabulary practice

The following words describe people in a positive or negative manner – sometimes it is difficult to say which. Group the words below in the correct boxes, then compare results with a partner to see if you agree. Try to find out the reasons for your choices.

competent	careful
outgoing	mean
cautious	silent
intelligent	creative
irrepressible	calm
serious	unimaginative
plodding	lively
vivacious	placid
cheerful	talkative

GOOD	BAD
careful	mean

Writing

1 Write a short description – not more than 200 words – of someone you know very well. Say what is good or not so good about them. Concentrate on their personality and not on their physical appearance. Remember when writing descriptions it is usually better to start with general observations or comments first, then progress to more specific detail.

2 The following newspaper headlines might have appeared over a number of days. Expand each idea and combine them into one story written for a magazine.

TWO-TIME MURDERER LEAVES DEATH ROW

Murderer seen on TV Chat Show

PRISON ROMANCE HAPPY ENDING

BATTERSEA WOMEN BEFRIENDS U.S. CONVICT

Trinidad mother flies to San Quentin

San Quentin bride flies home

TV CREW FILMS TEARFUL MEETING

I'M BROKE PLEADS TV JAIL WIFE

SON BACKS MOTHER FOR JAIL WEDDING

DIARY

pp. 18–21

Day(s) Date(s) Month Year

Texts

OK

Look at again

Ask the teacher

Look up in reference books

To remember

New Words

Grammar

Useful phrases

Unit 6

FOR BETTER OR WORSE
A Look At Marriage

Sometimes parents decide which partner is best for their son or daughter. Sometimes marriages go ahead more spontaneously.

Opening Discussion

Working in groups, draw up a list of reasons why you think people today marry. Arrange your list of reasons in order of importance. Each group can then present its findings and its comments to the class. Make notes while you are listening to the others.

Listening

You are going to hear comments from people about their motives for committing themselves to marriage. Fill in the chart while you are listening. You can also make a note of your own reaction to what they say.

Name	Reason	Your comments
Lisa		

Reading for information

Divide the class into two groups. Group 1 reads Part A and Group 2 reads Part B. Do not look at the other text!
Then make pairs, one from each group. Take it in turns to elicit the content of the text you have *not* read by asking as many questions as you need to.
Each student in turn must find out the content of the text the other has read by asking as many questions as necessary.
Students should then rejoin their groups and collectively recreate the other group's text using the information they have found. Finally, each group looks at the other text to check how accurate they were.

Part A

Gretna Green, a Historical Perspective

Towards the middle of the seventeenth century, attitudes to marriage began to change, largely due to pressure from the Puritans. Before this time, the majority of marriages had been arranged by the parents of the prospective bride and groom. It was not uncommon for children to be 'betrothed' at the age of seven!

Under the influence of the Puritans, moves were made to allow people to choose their own marriage partners for reasons other than financial gain or social status. They felt that the spiritual relationship between marriage partners was as important as the physical union. Nevertheless, there was still enormous parental pressure put upon young people to make the right choice.

Until 1836, marriage by licence was not permitted, which meant that everyone wishing to marry had to do so in church. There were one or two exceptions, however. Licences to perform marriages were granted to parsons of the Fleet Prison in London. Another was granted to the blacksmith in a village called Gretna Green on the Scottish border.

From 1770 onwards this location was very popular with young couples who had eloped for various reasons. Weddings used to take place in the smithy and could be performed by the blacksmith himself or the tollkeeper or the ferryman. Once the ring had been placed on the finger the marriage was legally valid. The bride and groom were almost always married in travelling clothes instead of the usual finery.

After 1856, an Act of Parliament made Gretna Green marriages invalid unless one of the couple had been resident in Scotland for a minimum of six weeks.

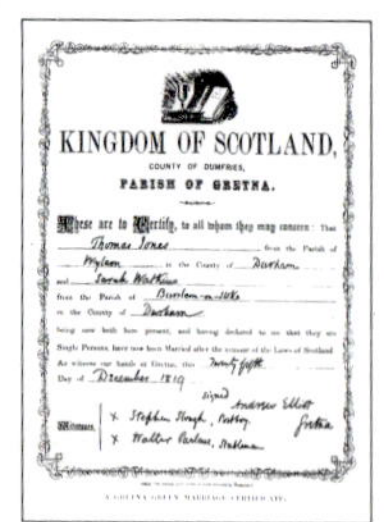

KINGDOM OF SCOTLAND,
COUNTY OF DUMFRIES,
PARISH OF GRETNA.

Check your understanding

Arrange these sentences in the order in which they happened.

1 Marriages were no longer made only to acquire wealth and position.
2 Couples were allowed to marry only in church.
3 Restrictions were placed on Gretna Green weddings from the mid-1850s.
4 People started to think differently about marriage.
5 Before 1836 only two places were allowed to marry people by licence.
6 Parents were responsible for choosing husbands and wives.
7 Marriage at Gretna Green became popular in the late 18th century.
8 Parents still exerted a great deal of pressure on their children.

Part B

Gretna Green, a Modern Perspective

Schoolgirl elopes to Gretna

Sandra Ross, a sixteen-year-old schoolgirl, has been disowned by her parents and dismissed from the position of Head Prefect by the headmaster of her school and all because she eloped to Gretna Green to secretly marry the man she loves.

Her parents, Arthur and Mavis Cook, have refused to talk to us. Her headmaster, Frank Jennings, had no comment to make, but Sandra is only too pleased to explain in this *Daily News* exclusive why she defied her parents to be with Peter Ross.

I was an only child. My parents have always given me everything. I have had all their love and anything else I asked for.

They sent me to a private school. When I was about thirteen I looked awful. I was overweight and quite plain so they sent me to a school for models. My mother bought me new clothes every week. I had a stereo, a video, a computer, loads of jewellery. Whatever I wanted. It was all too much.

I first met Peter three years ago. He had come with a workmate to instal my CB aerial. Last summer holidays I met him again by chance. We were on holiday in Bournemouth. I bumped into him on the beach one afternoon. He didn't recognise me at first because I had grown my hair long and had become blonde, lost a great deal of weight and had given up wearing glasses.

I felt he was so attractive. He has a very outgoing personality and is a lot of fun. There was a problem, though. I had been going out with another boy, Alex, for almost two years. He came from a very wealthy background and my parents liked him very much. Peter was from a totally different background.

I don't think my mother will ever forgive me for breaking up with Alex. She always insisted I could do better than Peter.

When we came back from holiday I called up Peter on my CB. He still had two weeks of his own holiday left and came to see me. It all began then. We used to go for long walks. It was so romantic.

My mother suddenly realised that we were not just having a holiday romance and started to make life difficult. She didn't want me to see him any more. She thought Peter was quite unsuitable and a bad choice. Peter was banned from the house and for two months she tried to stop us seeing each other. We did manage to meet but only with the help of friends. I had to be home by 10 o'clock every night.

Finally I was so desperate I ran away from home. Peter and I decided that we would like to spend our lives together so I went to live with a family he knows in Scotland. We were married three weeks later at Gretna Green. It was the only place we could think of where we could be married without my parents' consent.

I'm sorry that my mum never comes round to see me. I often feel that if I had been left alone we might not have done this. She ended up driving us into this situation which was precisely what she didn't want . . . an early marriage.

Check your understanding

Are these statements true or false?

1 Sandra Ross ran away to get married.
2 They had met thirteen years before.
3 Sandra at sixteen looked radically different from Sandra at thirteen.
4 Sandra's former boyfriend was from a similar background to her own.
5 Sandra heard Peter on the radio.
6 Sandra could see Peter with friends.
7 They needed their parents' consent to marry at Gretna.
8 Sandra's mother preferred Alex to Peter.

Adjectives + word order

In the news article, Sandra Ross tells us she had grown her hair long, become blonde, lost weight and had given up wearing glasses.
She could be described as a young, slim girl with long blonde hair.

1 When there are two or more adjectives describing a word, the most general is put first, followed by the most specific and objective.

eg a fine old house
a beautiful blue vase

2 If adjectives are equal, we begin with the shorter.

eg a quiet, intelligent student
a long, interesting story

3 Two equal adjectives are often joined by *and* for greater emphasis.

eg a bright and blustery day
a lively and interesting programme

Practice

Arrange the adjectives in brackets in the correct order before these nouns, then expand them into a sentence.

eg a girl (defenceless, poor)
⇒ a poor, defenceless girl
⇒ A poor, defenceless girl was standing in the snow selling matches.

1 an armchair (leather, luxurious, white)
2 a story (involved, ghost, spine-chilling)
3 a boy (handsome, sensitive)
4 a city (sprawling, modern, characterless)
5 the news (depressing, latest)
6 a stream (cool, clear, shallow)
7 a baby (pale, sickly, weak)
8 a dress (silk, blue, stylish)
9 a car (rusty, old, second-hand)

Now write three examples of your own and use them to test your partner.

By + until

We use *until* to talk about a situation or state that will continue up to a future moment.

eg Marriage by licence was not permitted until 1836.

By is used for an action that will (or will not) happen on or before a certain moment.

eg I had to be home by 10 o'clock every night.

Practice

Now try to decide for yourselves whether to use *until* or *by*.

1 I won't be coming to see you ______ the 7th of July.
2 Make sure that you have finished painting the house ______ next Wednesday.
3 Keep on doing the exercises ______ your stomach is flat.
4 I had finished my breakfast ______ the time you got up.
5 Make sure you have lost two pounds ______ weigh-in tonight.
6 Don't come home ______ you have learned some manners.
7 You have ______ the end of the month to pay the rent.
8 Pay the rent ______ the end of the month or else you're out.

Vocabulary practice

Fill in the gaps in the sentences with appropriate words from the box below.

engagement	bridal	wedding	best man	prospective	bride	couples
marriages	get married	marry				

1 The ______ walked down the aisle on her father's arm.
2 Many ______ no longer go to talk to the priest before the ceremony.
3 In many parts of the world ______ are still arranged by the parents.
4 In most European countries couples can ______ in a registry office as well as in church.
5 The bridegroom did not see his ______ bride on the night before the wedding.
6 By tradition the ______ carries the ring which he passes to the groom at the altar.
7 During the ______ ceremony music is played on the organ.
8 Hotels often have a special ______ suite for honeymooners.
9 Priests sometimes refuse to ______ divorced people.
10 These days, many people cannot afford to buy diamond ______ rings.

Writing

Write a description of a wedding. You can mention the ceremony, people present, special dress, the reception afterwards. Try to include the special traditions and customs of your country or, if the wedding you describe took place in another country, what differences did you find?

DIARY pp.22–25

Day(s) Date(s) Month Year

Texts

OK

Look at again

Ask the teacher

Look up in reference books

To remember

New Words

Grammar

Useful phrases

Unit 7

PARTNER vs PARTNER . . . When Things Go Wrong

There are as many reasons for the breakdown of a relationship as there are relationships. In spite of the rising divorce rate, thousands of couples get married every day and start life together full of optimism.

When problems do occur, however, many people take them to the Marriage Guidance Council where counsellors are available to offer advice and a sympathetic ear.

Listening

Before listening check the meaning of the following words.

munch	appalled	sore point	obsessive
keyboard	shuffle	shrug the shoulders	cocoon
whirlwind	romance	hygiene	
grotesque	screen	reconciliation	

While listening, make notes about what Mr and Mrs Masters each had to say on these subjects.

	Mr Masters	Mrs Masters
Working wife		
Hobbies/interests		
Character changes since meeting		
Personal appearance		
Communication		
Cooking and eating		
Mr Masters' job		
Children		
Divorce		

Role play

Put yourself in the position of the counsellor and her two colleagues and discuss what recommendations you should make to the couple next week. Use your notes on the husband and wife's main complaints in order to compare what each had to say and try to arrive at some conclusion. Prepare what you would say to them both together at the next meeting.

Act out your role play and the class can take a vote on whose approach seems to be the most effective.

Reading

Before you read the text,

1 Think about the following points.

   a Is there an ideal age to get married so that the relationship stands a chance of succeeding?

   b Does having children make any difference to a relationship?

2 Check the meaning of these words:

a law suit	to cite	testimony	to mete out	custody	to prohibit	ultimately

BOY, 14, WINS DIVORCE

A 14-year-old Tennessee schoolboy who was married at 12 and became a father at 13 joined the ranks of the divorced yesterday after winning a suit in which he cited the "cruel and inhuman treatment" meted out by his 17-year-old wife. For her part, the wife complained during testimony at the divorce hearing that during their short marriage her husband "behaved like a 10-year-old."

In granting the divorce at Gallatin, Tennessee, juvenile court, Judge Thomas Gray denied the boy, Hal Warden, custody of his 16-month-old daughter, Heather. The judge ruled that the child is to remain with the mother, Wendy Chappell Warden, and ordered Hal to pay her $30 (£22) a week in child support, plus all medical expenses not covered by insurance.

The boy, now in 8th grade at the local high school, was allowed annual visitation rights from Dec. 26 to Jan. 2 and June 15 to Aug. 5.

Devastating effect

The judge's ruling had a devastating effect on Hal. "My son is destroyed," said Herbert Warden, his father. "He collapsed in the doorway as he came in from school when I told him the news."

The elder Warden said he did not know how his son could afford the child support. He suggested he was being placed in a catch-22 situation. "State law prohibits Hal from taking a job at so young an age, but the court has ordered him to pay $30 each week. Where is he supposed to get that money? It will ultimately have to come out of my own pocket."

The pair met while Hal's family were living temporarily in Alaska. They were married on Jan. 20 1984, after Wendy learned she was pregnant. Heather was born four months later.

Check your understanding

Find out

Where – Hal and Wendy were married;
the divorce took place;
the child support money will come from.

Why – the relationship went wrong;
Hal is not able to earn anything.

What – the grounds for divorce were;
the child support amounted to;
custody arrangements were made;
a Catch-22 situation is.

Comment on

- the age of the couple;
- reasons for their marriage;
- parental attitudes;
- maintenance payments;
- the law which allows this to happen in the first place.

7 GRAMMAR GUIDE

Must + have to

Must and *have to* express obligation.

The essential difference is that *must* expresses the speaker's own self-imposed obligation, *have to* expresses an externally imposed obligation.
eg Hal had to pay $30 per week child maintenance.

Practice

Complete the sentences below with *must/mustn't* or a suitable form of *have to*.

1 You ________ come to dinner next week.
2 Visas ________ be arranged before you travel abroad.
3 We are making progress but we ________ forget that there are still a lot of problems to overcome.
4 That's a very difficult decision to ________ make.
5 Our car broke down on the motorway and we ________ have it towed to the garage.
6 You really ________ be so outspoken.
7 I was sorry to ________ tell her, but I had no alternative.
8 We ________ start planning our holiday route.
9 You ________ breathe a word about this to anyone.
10 Do you ________ make that awful noise?

Needn't + don't have to + don't need to

These forms express the absence of obligation.

Needn't generally expresses the speaker's own authority.
Don't have to / *Don't need to* } express (a) habitual actions; (b) something already planned or arranged.
Needn't have done expresses the absence of obligation in the past.

eg I needn't tidy my room if I don't want to.
You don't have to take the library books back till next week.
My friends didn't arrive, so I needn't have bought so much food.

Practice

1 Rewrite the parts of the sentences in brackets, using *needn't* or a suitable form of *have to* or *need to*, as in the example.

eg ⇒ (You're not obliged to) come just to please me.
You don't have to come just to please me.

a (It's hardly necessary for us to) tell you how grateful we are for all your help.
b They employed him on the spot. He (wasn't required to) fill in an application form or have an interview.
c (It's not necessary for you to) get upset.
d If only you'd listen (it wouldn't be necessary for me to) say things a dozen times.
e The meeting was really boring. (It wasn't necessary for me to) have gone.

Phrasal verbs practice

1 **GET** Fill the gaps in the sentences with one of the following phrasal verbs:
get on *get up* *get down* *get out*

- **a** In the morning the mischievous boy would ______ ______ to no good.
- **b** The two brothers didn't ______ ______; they couldn't stand each other.
- **c** Let's not waste any more time, let's ______ ______ to business.
- **d** Since the children were born we are finding it more and more difficult to ______ ______ at night.

2 **GO** Fill the gaps in each of the sentences with one of the following:
go on *go on* *go back* *go out*

- **a** I'm at the end of my tether, I feel I can't ______ ______.
- **b** I want to hear that bit again. Let's ______ ______ over it.
- **c** If you don't do the washing up, I won't let you ______ ______ tonight.
- **d** The teacher wouldn't leave the boy alone, she would just ______ ______ nagging at him all day.

3 **UP** Fill the gaps in each of the sentences with one of the following:
give up *set up* *write up* *end up*

- **a** Keep trying, there's no need to ______ ______ yet.
- **b** Look in your diary, we have to ______ ______ a meeting.
- **c** Take notes during the lesson and ______ them ______ at home in essay form.
- **d** If you don't go to the dentist, you'll ______ ______ with rotten teeth.

Mixed phrasal verbs

Complete each of the sentences below with one of the following phrasal verbs.
talk over *find out* *put down* *look after* *pick at* *come along*

1 Come and see me about your problem, and we'll ______ it ______ .
2 There's something funny here. I want to ______ ______ what's going on.
3 Yes, I'll make a contribution. ______ me ______ for £20.
4 I want to go to the theatre. Will you ______ ______ my baby brother tonight?
5 The princess didn't want to eat. She would just ______ ______ the food on her plate.
6 I'll be free at 6 o'clock ______ ______ and see me then.

Guided writing

'Getting married has to be made very difficult. Getting divorced needs to be made very easy.' Discuss the proposition in small groups and make notes on each person's ideas. Decide whether you support or oppose it. Plan and write a composition which gives a balanced view for and against, in not more than 500 words. Keep your own personal view until the final paragraph.

DIARY pp. 26–29

Day(s) Date(s) Month Year

Texts	**To remember**
OK	New Words
Look at again	
Ask the teacher	Grammar
Look up in reference books	Useful phrases

Unit 8

HOW GOOD A PARENT COULD YOU BE?

Perhaps you are a parent already, perhaps you are planning to become one. But how suitable are you for parenthood? Find out by doing this very revealing quiz . . .

Reading/discussion

Check these 'Good Parenthood' ratings. Answer the questions and look at the score chart on page 31. Test yourself and choose what you would do, then look through the questions again and assess your own parents – choose what they *actually* do! How different are the results? Compare results with your classmates.

Before you begin, make sure you know the meaning of these words and phrases. Check a dictionary of current usage, or ask your teacher.

prowl	vow	junk food	catch in the act
purloin	draining board	mug	
dregs	shimmer	sleuth	

Imagine you are the parent of a teenage daughter.

1 Your sixteen-year-old daughter goes out to a disco with friends and promises to be back home by 10.30 pm at the latest. It is 12.30 am, you are sitting on the stairs and she is still not back. (This is not the first time this has happened.) Do you:

- **a** Get in your car and prowl the streets in the hope that you will spot her?
- **b** Drive to the disco, pay eight pounds to get in and drag your daughter out screaming?
- **c** Trust to her good judgement?
- **d** Vow to cut her pocket money from next week?

2 When your sixteen-year-old daughter comes home from school she finds it absolutely necessary to telephone her girlfriend whom she last saw ten minutes ago. Your last telephone bill came to £274. Do you:

- **a** Have the phone disconnected?
- **b** Arrange for a payphone to be installed – and make her pay?
- **c** Instal a radio phone and carry the handset on a clip on your belt at all times?
- **d** Threaten to cut her pocket money?

3 As one of her household duties it is your sixteen-year-old daughter's job to do the family's ironing. After a while you notice that all your best tee-shirts and stripy long-sleeved shirts keep disappearing. She is purloining them for herself from all the members of the family. Do you:

- **a** Check through her cupboard to see if there is anything of hers you can take?
- **b** Do the ironing yourself?
- **c** Make your sons do the ironing?
- **d** Promise to cut her pocket money?

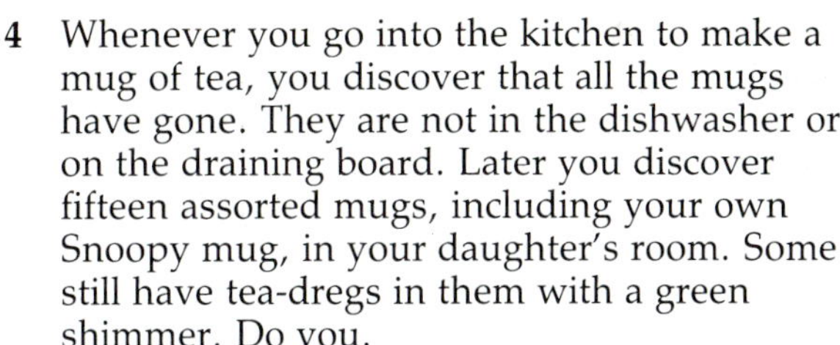

4 Whenever you go into the kitchen to make a mug of tea, you discover that all the mugs have gone. They are not in the dishwasher or on the draining board. Later you discover fifteen assorted mugs, including your own Snoopy mug, in your daughter's room. Some still have tea-dregs in them with a green shimmer. Do you.

- **a** Break all the mugs?
- **b** Hide the kettle?
- **c** Keep your Snoopy mug in your own bedroom?
- **d** Make a note to cut her pocket money?

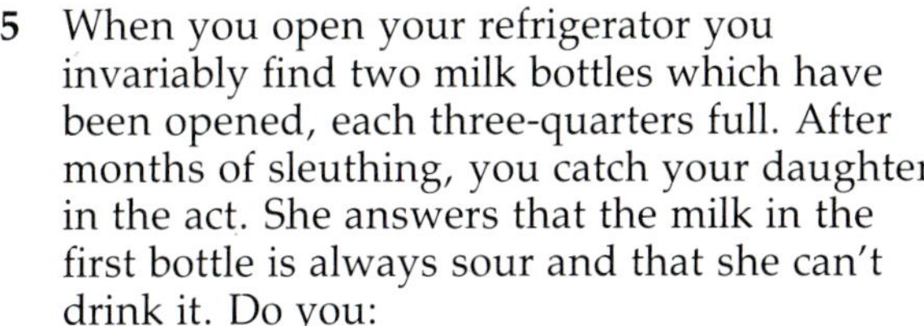

5 When you open your refrigerator you invariably find two milk bottles which have been opened, each three-quarters full. After months of sleuthing, you catch your daughter in the act. She answers that the milk in the first bottle is always sour and that she can't drink it. Do you:

- **a** Order only yoghurt in future and demonstratively take it in your tea?
- **b** Threaten to stop her pocket money?
- **c** Always open all the milk bottles as soon as the milkman delivers them?
- **d** Put a lock on the refrigerator door?

Now check your score

	A	B	C	D	Your Score
1	3	2	4	1	
2	2	4	3	1	
3	4	2	3	1	
4	2	3	4	1	
5	3	1	4	2	
				Total	

16–20: About right. You don't come down on your children too heavily and give them their head as individuals. Go on and have five!

11–15: Not so hot! You get pretty touchy, daughterwise. Why do you always insist on making a point? You are going to bring down a heap of trouble on your own head.

6–10: You are some kind of nut! This is precisely the kind of repressive behaviour that makes kids leave home! We suggest you take a Human Being Course!

5 or less: Do you think money solves everything? But thinking it over, you'll probably go far. You're probably too mean to have a kid in the first place.

Listening

Simon is the father of three teenagers. Listen to him talking about some of the difficulties. Make notes while you listen and then answer the questions.

- **a** Why did the fact that his eldest child started school fail to relieve the transport problem?
- **b** How many instruments did his children learn to play altogether?
- **c** What were the problems of having all three children learning the piano?
- **d** Find three reasons why the second son could not get to the school orchestra without the 'taxi service'.
- **e** What did the boys hope to learn at karate classes?
- **f** Do you think Simon likes being a parent?

Should + ought to + had better

Should and *ought to* are used when we make suggestions or recommendations.

eg Simon's daughter ought to be home by 10.30. She should telephone to say she'll be late.
Simon ought not to drag her out of the disco. He shouldn't cut her pocket money either.

Had better is used to suggest the wisest course of action in a particular situation.

eg Simon and his daughter had better sit down together and talk about their problems. They had better not get angry or upset.

When we want to comment on the past, *should* and *ought to* are used with a perfect infinitive. *Had better* can't be used for past time.

eg She should have told us she was going to be late.
They ought not to have given up their jobs without having others to go to.

Practice

1 Look back over the Good Parent Quiz.
Take each problem in turn and make your own suggestions, using *should, ought to* or *had better*.

2 Respond to these statements with constructive suggestions, using the words in brackets.
eg John's terribly overweight. (*diet*)

⇒ He ought to go on a diet.

- **a** The train leaves in less than half an hour. (*hurry up*)
- **b** My handbag's been stolen. (*report to police*)
- **c** We're going to Africa on a safari holiday (*buy a good camera*)
- **d** She stayed in the sun too long and was badly sunburnt. (*be more sensible*)
- **e** Paul has had another car accident. (*Give up driving*)
- **f** Steve is always complaining about his low wages. (*get a new job*)
- **g** There are so many people here that we'll run out of wine soon. (*buy a vineyard*)
- **h** They were caught in a thunderstorm yesterday and got soaked. (*carried an umbrella*)
- **i** These shoes of mine are falling to pieces and I've only worn them since last week. (*take back to shop*)
- **j** She's been looking very tired lately. (*get more sleep*)

Phrasal verb practice

In the following passage, phrasal verbs including *up* and *down* have been left out. Choose the right one from the following list and add verb endings if necessary:

take up   break down   give up   come down   throw up   wolf down   let up

Teenagers have atrocious eating habits. First they ____________ a diet, then they ____________ it ____________. They creep down the stairs at night into the kitchen, ____________ all the food they can find, then go into the bathroom and ____________. Parents should show iron determination and ____________ hard on them, but this resolution often ____________ and they have to ____________. The only thing is for them to ____________ mystic philosophy.

Vocabulary practice

8

1 Most of the following words have appeared in the last three units. Make them negative, using *un-*, *im-* or *in-*.

important	original	suitable	necessary
common	valid	expensive	demonstratively
cleanliness	sympathetic	provident	fortunately
easy	personal	accessible	

2 Which negatives from the list above fit the sentences below?

a ____________ lies the head that wears a crown.

b The edelweiss is a very ____________ flower in Holland.

c The city of Shangri-la lies in an ____________ valley in the Himalayas.

d It was ____________ of you to borrow so much money.

e Not only are your ideas ____________, they have also been shamelessly borrowed from an early work of mine!

Writing

This letter was sent to an Agony Aunt in a magazine. Your job is to write a reply offering advice.

Dear Heather

I have had a problem with my parents for a long time. They don't seem to want me to grow up. Whenever I need new clothes my mother goes shopping with me and bullies me into having things I really don't want.

I need to go on a diet since I am a pound-and-a-half overweight but they don't want to know. They insist on my eating great stodgy meals with meat and potatoes every evening and when I try to choose my own food they kick up a fuss. They have even threatened to put a lock on the refrigerator door! I am only thirteen and I can't leave home, but I am getting desperate. What Should I do?

Yours sincerely,

Marlene

pp. 30–33

DIARY

Day(s) Date(s) Month Year

Texts

OK

Look at again

Ask the teacher

Look up in reference books

To remember

New Words

Grammar

Useful phrases

9

Unit 9

A GOOD JOB WITH PROSPECTS

At one time people remained in the same job or profession for the whole of their working lives. But many change their jobs as better opportunities present themselves.

Listening

Bert is a sound engineer with BBC Radio. He is talking about his working life and what led up to his working with the BBC. While you listen take notes so that you can complete his personal dossier and answer the questions that follow.

Profile of a Career

Name: Bert

Job: BBC sound engineer

Secondary education: Grammar School

Qualifications: 5 'O'levels including ______ and ______

First employer: ______ ______ ______ ______

Annual salary: £______

Training: ______ ______ and evening classes

Further qualifications obtained: Physics 'A'level (failed ______ ______)

Length of service: Five years

Second employer: ______ ______

Training: RAF Trade Course

Qualification: ______ ______ ______

Position obtained: ______ ______ operator

Length of service: ______

Third employer: ______

Fourth employer: British Broadcasting Corporation

Name of job: ______ ______

Training: ______ ______ in-house training

Title after training: Sound engineer

Department: Recording Unit

Fifth employer: ______ Broadcasting Corporation (under secondment from British Broadcasting Corporation)

Further qualifications: Practical experience in ______ ______

Purpose: Technical assistance in expanding broadcasting service

Sixth employer: BBC, Training Department then BBC ______ ______ Broadcasts

Length of service: ______

Seventh employer: BBC, Outside Broadcasts

Check your understanding

1 Are these statements true or false according to the tape?

- **a** Bert became a scientist as soon as he left school.
- **b** He had hoped to escape spending time in military service.
- **c** He has always enjoyed working for the BBC.
- **d** He started to meet the beautiful, rich and famous when he first joined the BBC.
- **e** Bert didn't know anything about Outside Broadcasting until he went to East Africa.
- **f** He has to be prepared to work at any time.

2 Explain these words and phrases as used in the interview.

apprenticeship
on a probationary basis
I'd messed about with (recording machines)
broadened the horizons
manning control rooms
secondment
fundamental knowledge
pageantry
turned on (by)

3 Expand the following abbreviations.

BBC OB RAF TV

Reading

Read these quotations from the interview on tape and match each of them up to the job Bert was talking about, as in the first example. (You may need to listen to the tape again to check your answers.)

'I wasn't entirely happy about going back. Those two years away had broadened my horizons and made me restless.' __________

a 'I read an advertisement that they wanted Technical Assistants, so I applied.'

____

b 'In those days the whole idea was to get trained in order to put off your National Service by studying and getting a deferment – but finally they caught up with me.'

____

c 'I can't say that I met the beautiful, the rich and the famous at that time. The life of a probationary Technical Assistant doesn't rise to that.'

____

d 'There weren't any tape machines then. They had wire recorders. You did editing by knots. If the wire broke you just tied a knot in it and carried on.'

____

e 'I was trained as a Ground Wireless mechanic. We spent our lives on shift, manning this Control Room for military communications.' __________

f 'On the coast, a beautiful spot, typically sub-tropical, quite wonderful . . . it was fascinating for me to go to the other side of the world and live in a different culture.'

____

g 'I don't think that there is any doubt that the single most exciting event I have worked on is the outside broadcast of the visit of the Pope to Canterbury Cathedral . . . There was lots of interesting pageantry, that sort of thing, but it was technically very challenging. I got a lot of satisfaction from it.' __________

h 'You have to be available for work seven days a week. I can recommend outside broadcasting provided that you can handle the rather odd working conditions.'

____

GRAMMAR GUIDE

Adverbs

Adverbs modify verbs.

Adverbs of manner say *how* something happens.

eg We'll have to act quickly.

Many adverbs end in *-ly* but some have the same form as adjectives, eg *fast, loud, wide* and *hard*. (Some words ending in *-ly* are adjectives not adverbs. The main ones are *friendly, lovely, lonely, silly, ugly, cowardly, likely, unlikely*.)

Adverbs of place say *where* something happens.

eg The group is practising upstairs.

Adverbs of time say *when* something happens.

eg We are going to the bullfight tomorrow.

Practice

Make sentences using these adverbs.

angrily	fast	well	quietly
happily	slowly	badly	hard
noisily	suddenly	softly	nervously

Word order

When there are several adverbs in a sentence, the usual order in which they follow the verb is (1) *manner* (2) *place* (3) *time*.

eg They have been working (1) hard (2) in the garden (3) all day.

There are exceptions (of course!)

a When there is a verb of movement, the adverb of place is often put straight after the verb to complete the sense.
eg They walked to the cinema in a hurry last night.

b Adverbs of time are often put at the beginning of the sentence, particularly if it is a long sentence with other adverbs in it.
eg At two o'clock in the morning there was a loud knock at the door.

Practice

Place the adverbs in brackets in the correct place in the following sentences.

1. Thomas's birth was registered (in 1986, in Hounslow).
2. Take this package (immediately, to the airport).
3. Bert went to night classes (every evening, in Leeds, after work).
4. He came back (with his family, at 2 am, to the hotel).
5. They had been living (in East Africa, quietly, for two years).
6. Look (at the advertisement, carefully).
7. They came up (to town, a few months later).
8. Bert worked on (in that country, happily, for six more months).
9. We want to invite them (to the country, next year).
10. He was not caught up (fortunately, in the fighting).

Vocabulary practice

1 Fill in gaps in the following passage with suitable words.

_________ leaving school at the _________ of seventeen with only the bare _________ of qualifications, Bert wanted to _________ a scientist. His first job was as a laboratory assistant at a science college. He _________ some extra qualifications by attending night _________. After five years he was called _________ into the Royal Air Force, where he learned to be a radio mechanic and served in the Middle East. Afterwards he _________ back to his old job and worked a _________ two years there before getting a position with the BBC. He has been with this employer ever _________. He prefers sound radio to TV since this presents _________ of a technical challenge _________ him. He works _________ Outside Broadcasts and has worked on _________ important state occasions, most notably the _________ of the Pope to Canterbury.

2 Search for the hidden jobs.

A	F	D	G	H	N	S	M	C	X
A	C	H	J	O	E	N	E	P	I
V	B	I	C	R	S	W	C	O	E
Z	X	A	V	M	L	J	H	V	N
K	N	A	O	I	M	M	A	L	G
I	N	G	I	L	L	I	N	G	I
T	E	C	H	N	I	C	I	A	N
W	E	R	T	N	M	M	C	M	E
Z	X	C	V	B	N	M	N	L	E
O	P	O	P	E	R	A	T	O	R

DIARY pp. 34–37

Day(s) Date(s) Month Year

Texts

OK

Look at again

Ask the teacher

Look up in reference books

To remember

New Words

Grammar

Useful phrases

Unit 10

WORK

An Alternative View

Millions of capable and intelligent people are without work. Neither immediate nor longer-term solutions to the problem have been found. As a result, over the past few years, many new small businesses have appeared.

Reading

The text is in three parts. They are in the wrong order.

- Form three groups. Each group reads one part of the text only.
- Question members of the other groups to gather all possible information about the whole text. Answer the questions at the end.
- Put the three parts of the text into their correct order.

Before reading, try to explain the following words and phrases without using a dictionary.

engage the services of   PAYE   tax allowances   in the long term
venture   cottage industry   make a dent in

Part A

To attract clients Caroline put another ad in the local paper announcing her cleaning service and she also went from house to house placing leaflets through every door. This was paid for out of her own savings.

Since she had no experience of running a business Caroline made use of the Small Business Advisory Service. Under this scheme the Department of Employment engages the services of consultants who provide three free advice sessions for people new to business. They helped her start an accounting system but she complains that she was left to find out for herself about PAYE, National Insurance and tax allowances relating to the business.

After eight months, the business pays for Caroline's car and telephone, and she can draw a small salary for herself.

It is too early to say whether Caroline's venture will succeed in the long term, but it is difficult to see how an agency of forty part-time office cleaners can be a replacement for a 10,000 strong workforce of shipbuilders in North Yorkshire or how such 'cottage' businesses can make a significant dent in the 3 million unemployed figure.

Before reading, try to explain the following words and phrases without using a dictionary.

streaming   bread riots   woefully   moonlighter   politicians of all hues
at a stretch   'black economy'   plumbing

Part B

With each year the large employers in manufacturing industry grow fewer and fewer, and the sight of tens of thousands of workers streaming through the factory gates each morning becomes ever more rare. In certain parts of the country, particularly in the North East, three out of ten workers are unemployed. And yet somehow families seem to manage to survive for years at a stretch on woefully inadequate unemployment and social security payments. One theory is that this is only possible because of the 'black economy' or 'moonlighting' – engaged in by people doing work for cash, paying no social insurance or income tax, and thus featuring in no statistics of employment. These moonlighters do all kinds of things – plumbing, electrical repairs, small building work or window cleaning – and are paid in cash on the spot.

Not too far removed from the 'black economy', however, is the cottage industry on which so many politicians place their desperate hopes for providing the employment of the future. And indeed, cottage industries are growing. Official figures published in 1986 show that the labour force rose during the year by 342,000, of which 230,000 were self-employed.

One typical example of these new businesses is to be found in Northallerton in North Yorkshire. The 'Call a Cleaner' agency was set up to cover the whole of the North Yorks area.

Before reading, try to explain the following words and phrases by referring to the text.

compensate	on her books	overdraft facility	spurred	National Insurance

Part C

Although she had no experience of professional cleaning or of running a services agency, Caroline Cooper, 33, of Northallerton has shown that hard work and determination can more than compensate. Caroline was spurred into looking for an occupation which would make more money than the part-time teaching job she had been doing and which would keep her house and family going when her steelworker husband was made redundant last year. There seemed to be an opportunity to set up a cleaning agency and so Caroline applied for a licence from the Department of Employment which cost £115 and took six weeks to arrive.

In the meantime she had placed an advert for cleaners in the local paper (the ad cost £5) and held interviews. She took on 25 cleaners at first but now has 40 cleaners on her books. All of them are self-employed, pay their own National Insurance and provide their own cleaning materials, so it is difficult to see Caroline as their 'employer' in the traditional sense. But nevertheless, it is thanks to her organisational activity that they find work.

Check your understanding

1 What percentage of workers in the North East are unemployed?

2 Why don't certain workers appear in any employment statistics, and can you give a reason for the types of job that they do?

3 What size work force did Caroline Cooper at first recruit, and how long was it before she began to show a profit?

4 What gap in the market did Caroline identify?

5 What is the ratio of new jobs created by the self-employed and by employers?

Role play

Work in pairs: One of you is a prospective employer who has a cleaning agency and the other is an applicant for a job.

- Interviewer: think about the kind of information you need from the applicant.
- Applicant: give the information you think the employer wants.
- On the basis of the interview, decide whether you would employ the applicant *or* take the job.

10 GRAMMAR GUIDE

Relative pronouns

Relative pronouns are *who, whom, whose, which, that* and *what*.
Their most common use is to join two pieces of information together.

eg 1 What's the name of that man? He just came in.
⇒ What's the name of that man *who* just came in?

eg 2 I've found the book. You were looking for it.
⇒ I've found the book *that* you were looking for.

eg 3 This is Mrs Jones. You met her last month.
⇒ This is Mrs Jones *whom* you met last month.

eg 4 Susie married Edward. It made Peter very unhappy.
⇒ Susie married Edward *which* made Peter very unhappy.

eg 5 I saw an old man. His beard reached his waist.
⇒ I saw an old man *whose* beard reached his waist.

Practice

Combine these sentences using relative pronouns.

1 The new typist is very good. She came to work here last week.
2 Lake Windermere is probably the longest lake in England. It is only ten miles long.
3 I picked out a horse. It won the race.
4 Where are my shoes? I wore them this morning.
5 Jim can't come to the match. His wife is very ill.
6 That yellow car belongs to Brian. It has been badly damaged.
7 There's Janet Watson. You saw her at the last meeting.
8 The dish contained pieces of snake. You have just eaten it.
9 Mr Bishop was on the phone. His house is for sale.

Vocabulary practice

1 Match the job to the description.

plumber	acts as middle man between client and insurance companies
totter	looks after horses
nightwatchman	arranges concerts and entertainments
caretaker	instals and mends water and gas pipes
ostler	takes gamblers' bets on horses and dogs
night porter	searches through rubbish tips for sellable items
midwife	organises the cleaning of housing blocks or public buildings
bookmaker	guards public buildings and factories at night
impresario	helps mothers at childbirth
insurance broker	acts as hotel receptionist at night

2 Now make ten sentences from the words above, as in the example.
eg A plumber earns his money repairing water pipes.

3 Choose the correct word in brackets to fill the gaps in the following sentences.

a In the short-term new businesses are always faced with __________ problems.
(*money stream* *liquid money* *cash flow* *cash stream*)

b In the first place the finance is usually found from the owners' personal __________.
(*savings* *funds* *loan* *friends*)

c But sooner or later a more __________ solution has to be found.
(*short term* *long term* *quick term* *long period*)

d The first way is to seek an __________ from the bank manager.
(*loan* *investment* *advice* *overdraft*)

e But he will certainly want to see your ____________.
(*will* *mortgage* *identity card* *business plan*)

f Too many companies have gone ____________ in recent years.
(*mad* *bankrupt* *to their head* *overboard*)

g So the banks have to be careful in placing their ____________.
(*deposits* *withdrawals* *investments* *currants*)

h Only a good plan drawn up with the assistance of your ____________ will convince him.
(*bookmaker* *bookkeeper* *accountant* *priest*)

i Even then he will probably insist on your using your ____________ as security.
(*wife* *job* *house* *bank account*)

j But you must be very careful that you can afford to meet the ____________ of interest and capital. (*repayments* *reinvestments* *accrual* *charges*)

Pronunciation

Place the following words, taken mainly from Unit 10, into the correct boxes, not according to meaning but according to the pronunciation of *ea*.

reason	steak	years	leaflet	cleaning
break	ready	breakfast	create	appear
feature	early	bread	earnings	teapot
heard	steam	dead	teach	

early	feature	bread	break	?

DIARY

pp. 38–41

Day(s) Date(s) Month Year

Texts

OK

Look at again

Ask the teacher

Look up in reference books

To remember

New Words

Grammar

Useful phrases

Unit 11
WOMEN AT WORK

Opening discussion

Working in small groups, discuss the following points. Keep a record of your views in note form. You will need them later.

- Do you think women are better off than they were ten years ago?
- Is the act of achieving equality at work matched by the satisfaction gained from it?
- Have women's rights advanced equally throughout the world? If not, why not?

Reading

THE DECADE FOR WOMEN

In 1985 women from all over the globe gathered in Nairobi to take stock of the previous ten years, designated by the United Nations as the Decade for Women. And indeed, at first glance, looking around the world one could conclude that great progress had been made in improving the political, economic and social lot of women. The decade ended with at least half a dozen countries headed by women (but who remembers that it began with eleven countries whose governments were led by women?) Many countries – many developed countries – have been consolidating the equal rights and equal employment legislation fought for in the previous decade.

In certain countries, notably the United States, part of this fight for equality has meant women in the Armed Forces joining their male comrades on the battlefield, bayonet in hand, instead of merely performing support roles. Or, as Germaine Greer said of her visit to Cuba, 'Women who have been trained to kill will be wearing pearlised nail polish and lipstick when they do it.' This was hardly the explicit intention of early campaigners for equal rights.

But the picture which emerged in report

after report at Nairobi was one of almost unrelieved gloom. Women's advances in certain Western European countries and North America are sadly overshadowed by gross economic, social and legal injustices in the Third World. Women perform two-thirds of the world's work but earn only one tenth of income. As one American observer said, 'Thai farmers are known for their industriousness and high productivity . . . and sometimes their husbands even help'. In many countries, not only in Africa, the menfolk are forced into leaving home and moving to the cities in search of work, leaving the women to feed and fend for the family. Throughout much of the developing world, education is still a luxury reserved for boys. For every two male illiterates there are three women.

Without doubt the Decade for Women has focused attention on women's rights, although studiously ignored by the tabloid press, and in many countries organisations are working hard for the advancement of women. But the feeling of the Nairobi conference was that the time for talking is now over, and the next ten years will need concrete action.

Check your understanding

1 Match these words and phrases from the text to the correct alternatives opposite. The first has been done for you.

take stock of → assess	hard work
lot	unacceptable
consolidating	strengthening
bayonet	highlighted
gross	assess
injustices	look after
industriousness	deliberately disregarded
fend for	popular newspapers
focused attention on	discrepancies
studiously ignored	sharp blade
tabloid press	situation

2 Answer the questions.

- **a** What does Germaine Greer mean by 'Women . . . will be wearing pearlised nail polish and lipstick . . .'? (line 24–25)
- **b** What interest has the press shown in the Decade for Women?
- **c** What was the purpose of the conference in Nairobi?
- **d** What has equality meant to women employed in a military capacity in the USA?
- **e** Describe the Third World attitude to education when there are choices to be made.

Listening

Ruki Shillam is a former General Science teacher from Sri Lanka. Her qualifications include HNC (Higher National Certificate) in Applied Biology. She is now working as a chemical analyst during the week. On Saturdays she works the all-night shift on the switchboard of a London police station.

Life was very hard for Ruki when she first came to Britain. Listen and make notes, then complete the sentences below.

1 Ruki decided to look for paid employment when ______________________________.

2 Her dressmaking skills were tested by ______________________________.

3 Three of the tasks necessary to complete a blouse were ______________________________.

4 The going rate for making blouses then was __________ per garment; the current rate per hour is ______________________________.

5 Two reasons for Ruki being able to work only at night were ______________________________.

Points for discussion

- Why do you think women are prepared to tolerate these working conditions?
- Do you know of a similar situation in your own country? What are the rates of pay?
- Could anything be legally done to improve the situation of home-workers?
- If you had been given the job of making such improvements possible, how would you approach the problem?
- In your experience do women really do so much of the work in the world?
- If women do so much work why do you think they earn so little?

Working with words

Word building I

Choose the right verb prefix from the box below to fill each of the gaps in the following passage. (Sometimes no prefix is necessary.)

di-	in-	per-	de-	sub-	re-	en-	re-	de-	e-	(none)

After the medical inspection, the army volunteer felt really ______jected. He was convinced that the panel had ______jected him. However, to his surprise, he was accepted. The new recruits were told by the sergeant to ______form up in lines and they were marched to the station where they were to ______train. He thought that he would be ______trained for the first ten weeks but it ______merged that they were going straight to the front. In the carriage were some cavalrymen who had been ______trained as infantrymen, much to their disgust. Near the front the railway lines from different directions ______merged into one. On the platform the recruit felt ______merged in a sea of humanity. A cook was trying to ______fend off the hungry soldiers and ______fend his pots of stew. He ______formed a minor miracle, however, and fed most of them without a riot. The recruit ______vested part of his first week's pay in a packet of cigarettes and after ______vesting himself of his baggage, sat behind a wall and lit one.

Word order

In these sentences the words have been scrambled. Sort them out and place them in the correct order.

tabloid over studiously the the ignored years movement press has women's the

case night children in only to in were any work after the I bed able at was

women are cheap of daily as labour everywhere being thousands exploited

trained kill polish who when they women do it lipstick and wearing have nail been will to be

Word building II

Fill the gaps in the following sentences with the correct noun form of the adjective in brackets, using one of the suffixes from the box below.
eg generous ⇒ generosity

-ment	-ness	-cs	-ity	-ety	-my

1 Pressure groups often campaign for social ________. (*equal*)
2 The left-wing ________ of the local party have changed a great deal since the last election. (*political*)
3 The future well-being of a country depends on a sound ________. (*economic*)
4 The ________ of a document is sometimes doubtful. (*legal*)
5 The ________ of her letter left us in no doubt that she was telling the truth. (*explicit*)

6 They are not related, but their __________ in every respect is quite surprising. (*similar*)

7 The new town centre __________ promises to be a very interesting piece of urban architecture. (*developed*)

8 The women of today hope that the __________ of tomorrow will offer them greater equality. (*social*)

Making sense

Ruki often spoke in a very condensed manner in her interview. Replace the underlined words with a suitable alternative from the words in brackets.

eg Always I would look out for these things with 'Machinist Wanted'.
(*jobs newspaper advertisements positions*)

Answer: *newspaper advertisements*

1 I used to do the children's dresses. (*sell make buy*)
2 They decide whether you are the sort they need. (*the right-aged worker the type of worker the right sex of worker*)
3 A minute later he produced all these blouses. (*manufactured acquired brought out*)
4 My mother produced some really nice blouses. (*brought out manufactured polished off*)
5 Her children were out at school and she had all day.
(*had to work all day had all day to work had the day off*)

Guided writing

The following headlines might have appeared in a Third World newspaper over a period of three years. Using the headlines, expand the story and re-tell it in non-journalese English. The story need not be set in Africa. You can place it anywhere where you think it likely to happen.

20TH CENTURY HITS AFRICAN VILLAGE

Village elders plan new pottery kiln

EEC VISITORS FOR MODEL PROJECT

DEVELOPMENT GRANTS FOR MONEY-MAKING PORCELAIN PLAN

NEW WORK SCHEME ON SCHEDULE

Business as usual for pottery women: 2-mile hike from well to kiln

POTTERY SCANDAL REVEALED; ENGINEERS FORGOT WATER SUPPLIES

Pottery production figures shock

DIARY		pp. 42–45
Day(s) Date(s)	Month Year	
Texts	**To remember**	
OK	New Words	
Look at again		
Ask the teacher	Grammar	
Look up in reference books	Useful phrases	

Unit 12

WORKFORCE 2000

The nature of work and our attitude towards it have been changing since the Industrial Revolution. Can we adjust to the new conditions of work?

Opening activity

- Working in groups, compile a list of questions which will help you to find out the reasons why people work (eg money, satisfaction etc) and how they might feel if they were not able to work.
- Put the questions to each member of the group in turn and write down the answers.
- Now compare your answers with those of the other groups. Draw up a list of similarities and differences. Can you see any pattern in people's attitudes?

Listening

Dennis is talking about his experience of unemployment. While you are listening, make notes about the circumstances in which he became unemployed. Try to work out his attitude to being without a job and how it compares with the results of your survey above. Do you think he represents a typical sample of the working population?

Reading

The text has been divided into three parts. Form three groups. Read *one* part each.

Within your group, ask each other questions to test understanding of the text and vocabulary. Discuss your section of the text. Pick out the main points. Tell each other what it is about in your own words.

Work . . . what do we mean?

Part A

In historical times, many societies operated a two-tier system made up of those who controlled and those who worked and were controlled. Work was not thought to be a desirable pursuit. However, another group of people emerged alongside this system. They were the merchants and artisans. Merchants worked for profits, artisans for wages. These were the people who first gave us the idea of work as paid employment.

Today people seem to need to work in the same way that they need to eat and drink. This is what we call the 'work ethic'. People work for the money they need in order to live well, but there is another reason beyond that basic motivation which makes people want to work.

In a pre-industrial society the work ethic did not exist. Work and leisure went together and only part of Sunday was taken as time off. In this society, singing, talking, drinking and gossiping went on together with work. With the emergence of the work ethic came the separation of leisure and holidays from the former ordinary social system of interaction. During the Industrial Revolution, work for most people was so unpleasant that leisure was regarded as a kind of freedom. Yet in spite of the fact that life was so hard and the nature of the work so arduous, people slowly changed from *having* to work to *wanting* to work.

Check your understanding

1. What was the difference between the work motivation of merchants and artisans?
2. Explain the concept of the 'work ethic'.
3. What is the meaning of 'the former social system of interaction' (line 23)?
4. Why do you think that in historical times work was not thought to be a desirable pursuit?

Part B

They now live to work rather than working to live. Work gives people a feeling of being useful but still there are many people who very much dislike their jobs. Their usefulness is synonymous with paid employment. The ethic runs so deeply that people today feel it is their right to work.

The question we should perhaps be asking ourselves is, firstly, whether we really like our jobs and secondly, even if we do like them, whether they are really necessary.

Many kinds of work are disappearing as natural resources are used up and new technologies appear. Computers are already replacing people to do boring repetitive jobs and improve efficiency. To a large extent, the price of labour, as compared with the cost of the new equipment, determines which jobs will be replaced. However, the new technologies will themselves generate new jobs both in the computer field and in the leisure industry.

It has been predicted that new technology could engineer a period of growth and prosperity. This does not mean that the ever-growing number of unemployed will drop. What it does mean is that finance and resources will become available to change the division between the haves and the have-nots. Large sums could be poured into social services, education and the health service. The quality of life could be substantially improved with better facilities and a significant increase in the workforce behind the services.

Check your understanding

1 How is modern technology reducing the workforce?

2 In which industries will the same modern technology generate more work?

3 What do you understand by the expression 'the haves and the have-nots' in lines 59–60?

Part C

It has taken well over a hundred years to reduce the working week from 60 to 55 hours, then 48, 44 and now 40. The next two steps will be a reduction to 35 then perhaps 32 hours. The current five-day working week will become a four-day or even a three-day event. Paid holidays are likely to increase and the age of retirement is likely to be lowered. In order to achieve this shortened working span, attitudes to work must be revolutionised. We have to try to get back to the usefulness ethic which prevailed before the Industrial Revolution. Community and caring ought to be brought to the fore, and the leisure industry needs to be expanded to cater for the needs of young and old alike, all of whom will have more spare time. In Europe, only France has taken this problem seriously enough to appoint a senior government official responsible for 'free time'.

Education for life and for a lifetime can provide many answers. Creativity and sensibility could generate a whole new era, perhaps a new Working Renaissance.

Check your understanding

1 In what way is the working year of the future to be reduced?

2 What was the length of the working week over a century ago?

3 Explain the term 'Working Renaissance' in lines 85–86.

4 Why do you think no country other than France has appointed a government official responsible for 'free time'?

Project

Working either alone or in small groups, collect data and give a short presentation based on the work situation in your own country. You could talk about employment or training schemes, future propects for the unemployed and the employed alike. Illustrate your talk with charts or recordings.

GRAMMAR GUIDE

Impersonal it*: preparatory subject*

> When an infinitive or a 'that' clause is the subject of a sentence, it does not normally start the sentence. We more often begin with *it* and put the real subject later.

eg It has been predicted that new technology could engineer a period of growth and prosperity.
This kind of structure can express many different ideas. Some examples are:

Time
eg It took me two hours to get here.

Emotions
eg It was wonderful to see him again.
It would be a great pity not to go.
It was surprising that she knew nothing about him.

Possibility
eg It is possible that the work may take less time than anticipated.
It is probable that they'll turn up late.

Importance
eg It is important that I speak to the Director at once.
It is essential to finish the work on time.

Practice

Look at the following phrases. Decide what ideas they express then add a suitable ending to complete the sentence. (Some are similar to the examples above, some are quite different.)

1 It suddenly occurred to me that . . .
2 It is obvious that . . .
3 It is pointless to . . .
4 It is customary to . . .
5 It must be very difficult to . . .
6 It was lovely to . . .
7 It is true that . . .
8 It was unimaginable that . . .
9 It would suit us both to . . .
10 It is quite likely that . . .

Prepositional verbs

Look at the following prepositional verbs. Try to think of a way in which each is used. Then choose suitable verbs from the box to fill the gaps in the sentences below. Each verb is used only once.

pour into	look for	look round
arrive at	pay into	divide into
apply for	go up	take on
	distinguish between	

1 In every cloud you should ________ ________ the silver lining.

2 Now, children, ________ the plasticine ________ three lumps.

3 In this haze it is difficult to ________ ________ sky and sea.

4 When you get the cheque ________ it ________ my account, please.

5 I cannot keep on ________ money ________ your crazy schemes!

6 Two people came to ________ ________ the house.

7 Inflation is set to ________ ________ by only three per cent this year.

8 With things the way they are I cannot see myself ________ ________ any new workers this year.

9 How on earth did you ________ ________ that conclusion?

10 One hundred people have ________ ________ this position.

Brush up your past irregular verbs

Change the verbs in brackets into the correct form of the past tense to complete the story.

On the cliff-face the climber (cling) on for dear life. He (swing) perilously on a single rope. At last he (find) a toehold and, by chance, a tree-stump. He (wind) an end of the rope around it, (bind) it fast and (hang) from it. Inch by inch he (slide) down the rope. He paused and (light) a cheroot. A smile (come) over his face. The climber casually (hold) on with one hand, (fling) the match away, (stick) the cigar between his lips and confidently (shoot) down to the bottom.

DIARY			pp. 46–49
Day(s)	Date(s)	Month	Year
Texts		**To remember**	
OK		New Words	
Look at again			
Ask the teacher		Grammar	
Look up in reference books		Useful phrases	

Unit 13

THE LEISURE INDUSTRY

Tens of thousands of good-humoured cyclists take part each year in a charity ride from London to Brighton.

Opening activity

Can you identify these cycles? Label the drawings correctly from the list below.

tandem
penny-farthing
unicycle
tricycle
sit-up-and-beg bike
butcher's bike
city bike
racing cycle

- Do you do any cycling? Can you think of any reasons why it should be preferable to motor racing as a sport?
- Draw up a list of the relative advantages and disadvantages of travelling by bicycle over motor travel.

Listening

Make notes while you listen and answer the following questions:

1 How popular is marathon running world-wide?
2 Name two events which the people of London support in large numbers.
3 Why do you think the Brighton Bike Ride gets little publicity?
4 While the cyclists are gathering why are the streets so quiet?
5 Describe three types of cyclist who take part.
6 What kind of support do they get *en route*?
7 Why is Ditchling Beacon such an obstacle?
8 Describe the kind of clothes serious cyclists normally wear.

Reading

The headlines from the following newsclips have been removed. Scan the texts and match the headlines to the appropriate news items.

1

There were ugly scenes this morning when cycling marshals escorted from the starting line an eight-man team from the West Country that had been disqualified. Protesting that there was no rule stating that eight-man teams were not allowed to take part in the event, Devon man Daniel Widden demanded reinstatement. Stewards were adamant, however, and insisted that a horse cannot be considered a bicycle in the normal meaning of the term.

VETERANS PROTEST RACE

Brighton Run Latest

2

'I'm all washed up,' gasped 80-year-old novice cyclist Clarence Brown from Ashby-de-la-Zouche. 'It really knocks it out of you. It's not so much the hills as the gallons of Women's Institute tea those ladies keep pouring into me. My insides must be as wrinkled as a prune! I'll never do it again. I swear!'

3 Glamorous, petite WPC Sandra Smythe (39), known as the 'Juliet Bravo' of the 3-man strong Detling police force was knocked down and not seriously hurt when the brakes failed on the bicycle ridden by veteran grandma cyclist, Mrs Elsie Sidebotham, who careered backwards down the main road.

SEVENTH MAN ON A BIKE

TEAM DISQUALIFIED

4 The ghosts of the last trams to run from Clapham to Streatham haunted the annual cycle rally to Brighton this morning. Four hundred front wheels were buckled beyond repair when they slipped into the old tram tracks which had been filled in with tarmac when the service was shut down in 1947. Police theorise that the tarmac was worn away by the wheels of the first 25,000 cyclists to go by.

5 'Riding to Brighton? It's a doddle!', says 23-year-old Peter Gurney, who rides last man on a bicycle made for seven. 'Why, I haven't even learned to ride a bike. I just put my feet up and let them do all the work. I can't think why I bother to go at all, actually.'

Devon Man all washed up

6 Violence struck again at the normally peaceful Brighton Bike Ride when a group of veteran Car Rally drivers drove their Bugattis into the road to block the cyclists' path. Twenty cyclists piled head-down into the obstruction but fortunately none was hurt since they were all wearing safety belts. 'We were protesting at the cyclists using our route', said the drivers. 'We want all the publicity to ourselves.'

7 Of the 25,647 cyclists who started out from Clapham Common this morning in the annual Brighton Bike Ride, only 647 had finished the fifty-mile course by six o'clock this evening. It is estimated that the remaining 25,000 participants will drift in slowly this evening after the pubs shut.

TRAMS SABOTAGE CYCLISTS

WPC Hit by Runaway Granny

Now answer the questions below.

1 Why was the West Country cycling team disqualified? Do you think the disqualification was fair?
2 How experienced a cyclist was Clarence Brown?
3 What do you think the Women's Institute is?
4 Which direction was Elsie Sidebotham travelling in when she had her brush with the police?
5 In the collision between cyclists and veteran car owners, how many cyclists were hurt? What was the reason for this?

Explain the meaning of the following words and phrases as they are used in the text.

careered
It really knocks it out of you
drift in
beyond repair
theorise
ugly scenes
reinstatement
adamant
to pile into an obstruction

GRAMMAR GUIDE

Expressing preferences

If you talk to any cyclist, they are quite likely to tell you that they prefer cycling to any other sport.

> **1** An *-ing* form after *prefer* is most often used to talk about general preferences.

eg 'Do you like skating?'
'Yes, but I prefer skiing.'

1 Working in pairs, ask each other questions and express preferences on the following topics: water sports *eg* swimming, diving; holidays; outdoor activities; hobbies.

> **2** When we talk about preferences on a particular occasion the infinitive is used.

eg 'Would you like me to go with you?'
'No thanks, I'd prefer to go alone.'

2 Working in pairs, expand the prompts to ask and answer questions as in the example.

. . . a lift home?	No, . . . walk.
. . . eat out?	No, . . . stay/home.
. . . see/film?	No, . . . go/other time.
. . . drive/Scotland?	No, . . . travel/train.
. . . go/camping?	No, . . . stay/hotel.

> **3** *Prefer* can be used with an infinitive. We can then add another clause with *rather than*.

eg 'Shall we visit my mother on Saturday?'
'I'd prefer to spend the weekend at home, rather than go to your mother's'

3 Working in pairs again, ask and respond in a similar way, using these cues.

buy/motorbike	spend/money/washing machine
take/trip/coast?	go/walking/country
spend/evening/Joe and Ellen?	stay/home
get tickets/musical?	see/serious play
take/sister/dinner?	eat/home

> **4** Asking questions: When we ask people directly about their preferences we can use *prefer* + inf. or *rather* + bare infinitive.

eg Would you prefer to stay here or keep going? *or*
Would you rather stay here or keep going?

4 Working in pairs, ask and respond, using the cues below and either *would prefer to* or *would rather*, as in the example. (Note that with *eat* and *drink* the infinitive after *prefer* can be omitted.)

eg 'Would you prefer (to eat) steak or fish?'
'Oh, I'd much rather have fish, thanks.'

(drink) red/white/wine	learn Russian/Spanish
see/tennis/football match	travel/air/car
go home/stay longer	
play squash/tennis	

Past tense practice (Irregular Verbs)

Change the verbs in brackets into the appropriate form of the past tense.

The cyclist (swing) a leg over the saddle, waited for the signal and then (speed) off. The Frenchman (lead) for the first day and won the Yellow Jersey. Then the Russian (take) over the lead. In the mountains there was a collision. The Russian (fall), cut his shoulder and (bleed) over the sweater. We (read) in the newspapers that the Frenchman (get) the red and yellow jersey back on the fourth day. The rest of the field (string) out over France. But finally a Belgian (take) the lead and (wring) victory from the French team. His face (shine) as they sprayed champagne over him. At last he had (win) the coveted jersey.

Gap test

The following extract from the Bike Ride route has had some words removed. Complete the text using the words in the box below. Use each once only!

just	before	rest	along	straight	into
top	travel	fork	past	cross	chance
up	turn	by	keep	mad	take

Turn right in Wivelsfield and then left at Ote Hall Chapel. ________ the railway at Ditchling Common to Ditchling. ________ extra care on Ditchling Common main road – it's very busy and quite hilly so ________ in single file.

Leave the village, ________ left up Beacon Road and keep ________ on at the foot of the Beacon. Just here is your last ________ for a welcome cuppa and sandwich ________ the infamous Ditchling Beacon. This stop is provided for us ________ the good old Ditchling Scouts again.

At the ________ of the Beacon there is a field to ________ in. From the top of the Beacon ________ going straight on to the junction, turn left and immediately right ________ Coldean Lane, ________ Hollingbury Hill, to the edge of Brighton itself!

Take care – don't go ________ on the last leg of the ride. Go down Ditchling Road and ________ St Peters Church. Go ________ the Steyne to the Palace Pier. Now ________ left into Madeira Drive and it's ________ half a mile to the finish line. 56 miles – well done!

DIARY pp. 50–53

Day(s) Date(s) Month Year

Texts	**To remember**
OK	New Words
Look at again	
Ask the teacher	Grammar
Look up in reference books	Useful phrases

Unit 14

SPORT AND THE TRIBAL INSTINCT
Football Hooliganism

Football is a sport that has a long and colourful history. There is a theory that its origins are in some way responsible for today's violence.

Listening

Read the following questions before listening to the interview. Make notes as you listen, then answer the questions.

1 How far back can games resembling football be traced?
2 How did the Romans come to play football?
3 What kind of ancient festivals are thought to have some connection with the game of football?
4 Why did it become necessary for some English kings to try to ban football, and what was the result of this?
5 What form does a modern Shrove Tuesday game take?

Group task

In small groups conduct your own sports survey. Question a number of people (starting with the class) to find out which sports people play and which they watch.

Jig-saw reading

The reading text has been divided into four parts, which are not in the correct order. The class should form four groups, each of which reads *one* part of the text. Practise telling each other what the text is about, then choose one spokesperson to tell the other groups about your part of the text. Make notes as you listen. Scan all four parts then decide what order they should be in.

WHAT CHANGED THE FRIENDLY FACE OF FOOTBALL?

A

One man who documented these changes is Geoffrey Green, former chief soccer correspondent of *The Times*.

Green says he noticed a difference in the behaviour of the crowds from the time National Service was abolished in 1960, and the younger elements seemed to become ill-disciplined.

'But the growth of crowd violence happened quite slowly. It started to become "fashionable" 25 years ago, when gangs chose soccer grounds as their stage, just like the gangs in *West Side Story* taunting each other from their territories.'

But Green observed other changes taking place, too.

'Jimmy Hill,' he says, 'is responsible for one particular change. As chairman of the Professional Footballers' Association, he negotiated higher wages for players, leading to Johnny Haynes becoming the first £100-a-week player. What Jimmy probably didn't realise was that this would drive a wedge between the players and their supporters. Suddenly footballers became elite, living in expensive houses, driving to matches in flashy cars, no longer men-of-the-people. The top people got themselves literary agents, and began turning out books.

'Supporters were having to find £2 or £3 for a ticket instead of just a few bob, so they began to demand a greater quality of entertainment. If they didn't get it, they became resentful and the mood at grounds turned ugly.'

B

Former FA Secretary Sir Stanley Rous is one of British soccer's most respected figures. Now aged 90, he has seen how fan and player have become separated – first by income bracket, then by a ring of armour-clad police.

'It wasn't soccer that changed, it was society,' says Sir Stanley. 'When I was a lad, growing up in Suffolk, we respected authority – everyone from the village bobby to the local soccer referee. Hooliganism? Never heard the word mentioned.

'Soccer was mainly a working man's game. All week, in factories and offices throughout the country, the talk was about the next match. Then, on the big day, huge, good-natured crowds would set out from miles around for the ground.

Previous to this, in 1923, Stanley Rous was a steward in the Royal Box for the first Wembley Cup Final, when the crowd invaded the pitch because too many people had tried to cram into the stadium.

'A single policeman on a white horse kept order, and directed thousands back to their places,' says Sir Stanley. 'There was no ill-feeling of any kind.'

Sir Stanley was FA Secretary from 1934 to 1961, the period in which the greatest changes took place. Boots changed shape, the ball changed colour, players' wage-packets bulged, floodlights became the norm, and facilities for spectators became less spartan.

C

Green credits Jimmy Hill – when he was chairman of Coventry – with initiating another major change that this time may benefit the supporters themselves: the marketing of soccer as family entertainment.

'Many clubs, Luton and Watford in particular, are providing better, more comfortable facilities, so Mum and the kids can become soccer fans along with Dad. If it works, and something must first be done about terrace violence, it will herald a new, better era for the football supporter.'

Working towards the new era is The National Federation of Supporters Clubs. Formed 58 years ago, its activities have intensified recently to provide more comfort for fans. 'If people are well-treated they are less likely to cause trouble,' says NFSC general secretary Malcolm Gamlen.

Current Football Association general secretary Ted Croker approves. 'In the federation we have an ally which we know shares all our hopes and ambitions for the future of football,' he says. 'It stands for commitment – to individual clubs and to the game in general – for friendship and sportsmanship. I look forward to the day when the thousands who love football, but are staying away, will come flooding back. All of us who love football will welcome them back with open arms.'

D

Once upon a time, fans and players walked together to matches. In pubs, afterwards, they would discuss the game. The heroes would have their backs slapped and be treated to pints. Those who had played badly would get stick and several rounds of free advice.

That was almost a century ago, when the Football League was in its infancy. Then, to be a football supporter meant you belonged to a community embracing knowledge, pride and solidarity. Today, sadly, to be a football supporter means, to an unruly minority, being a *Hooligan*.

In the light, particularly, of the disaster at the European Cup Final in Brussels, coupled with coverage given by the press and television, a majority of the British public is ready to believe that football hooligans are simply drunken thugs, unemployed and socially inadequate. That, perhaps, is too simple an answer. For the past five years a team of sociologists from Leicester University has studied the social roots of football spectator violence.

Violence, as well as safety – because of the notorious fire at Bradford City's ground in which 56 people died – prompted the recent report by Mr Justice Popplewell. Among other things, it recommended a membership system for supporters and increased police power at games to combat violence. Only time will tell if these measures will be enough to put an end to football's ugliness.

GRAMMAR GUIDE

Conditional I

We often discuss problems which have fairly obvious solutions and outcomes. The conditional is often divided into three groups. Conditional I has this formula:

IF	PRESENT	FUTURE
If	*I buy* that house	it *will cost* a lot to repair it.

It is talking about cause and effect.

Practice

1 Complete the following sentences using the appropriate form of verbs in brackets.

eg If the clubs ______________ football up, people ______________ going to see it. (*not clean, stop*)

a If they ______________ special passes, it ______________ to attend the game. (*issue, become safer*)

b If the clubs ______________ the grounds up, fathers ______________ their children to matches again. (*clean, take*)

c If they ______________ beer in the stadium, spectators ______________ so wild. (*not sell, not get*)

d If they ______________ the stands more fireproof, there ______________ no more disasters. (*make, be*)

e If the courts ______________ the hooligans into prison, everyone ______________ a sigh of relief. (*throw, breathe*)

f If the visitors ______________ Millwall, there ______________ rioting in town tonight. (*beat, be*)

g If the ferries ______________ to carry football supporters, there ______________ no problem in Belgium this time. (*refuse, be*)

2 Now make up your own endings to the following sentences:

eg If it rains on Saturday ______________________________.

a If they buy that old car ______________________________.

b If we save a lot of money this year ______________________________.

c She will come on holiday with us if ______________________________.

d If I telephone the station ______________________________.

e They will reserve seats for the show if ______________________________.

f We will be able to see him ______________________________.

g If he leaves here before the rush hour begins ______________________________.

h If you give me your phone number ______________________________.

i I will get up early ______________________________.

j He will go to France ______________________________.

Project

The Listening section of this unit is about the history of football. Working in small groups, choose another sport and find out as much as you can about its origins. Use the guide below to help you organise the information.

Ancient times

- **a** religious/superstitious connections (if any)
- **b** any details which are similar to the modern version of the sport
- **c** how it came to your country and when

Developments or changes

- **a** Was it always popular?
- **b** Was it forbidden at all?
- **c** How was it absorbed into festivals or traditions in your country?

The game today

- **a** Commercial interests
- **b** Personalities
- **c** Fashions
- **d** Support and participation
- **e** Any hangovers from the past?

Your local library reference section is always a good place to begin looking for the information. You could also try contacting the secretary of a local sports club or reading back issues of sporting journals.

Present your findings to the class, then write a summary of your report in not more than 400 words.

Vocabulary

Match each of the verbs on the left with the correct sport on the right. Only one answer is correct in each case.

shoot	baseball
punch	golf
throw	fishing
strike	sailing
bowl	football
pass	climbing
serve	snooker
pot	cricket
drive	boxing
jump	swimming
stem	parachuting
cast	wrestling
tack	skiing
crawl	tennis
abseil	rugby

DIARY pp. 54–57

Day(s) Date(s) Month Year

Texts

OK

Look at again

Ask the teacher

Look up in reference books

To remember

New Words

Grammar

Useful phrases

15

Unit 15

LOST AND DISTRESSED

When first visiting a foreign country or an unfamiliar city, the fear of getting lost can be a major concern and everyone has a tale to tell.

Listening

The Bull Ring

This true account concerns the city of Birmingham in England, but it could happen equally in any city in the world that has undergone a modernisation and rebuilding programme. Before listening, check the meaning of these words.

suburb	to depict	desolate	flyover	maze	to spot	take one's bearings
precinct	ample	to bound				

Now answer the questions.

1 Find words or phrases in the story which refer to

- **a** looking (*eg* 'note')
- **b** movement up or down
- **c** things unknown
- **d** parts of the structure of the city centre development

2 Complete these sentences.

- **a** The speaker volunteered to drive his sisters to the concert . . .
- **b** The 'Bull Ring' was not . . .
- **c** The development complex consisted of . . .
- **d** The speaker was worried that . . .

3 Why were local people, including a policewoman, unable to help?

Pair work

Listen to the speaker's description of the city centre of Birmingham. The following places are all mentioned in the recording and are shown by numbers on this picture of the area. Identify the places.

- **a** Car park
- **b** Skyscraper
- **c** Shopping precinct
- **d** Subway
- **e** Circular urban motorway

Group work

Have you ever been lost in a strange town? Write down where and how it happened and what you did to get out of the situation. Tell the group about it.

Do you think finding your way is easier or more difficult in a modern city centre development than in an old town?

Reading

Before reading, look up these words.

frayed	casual	poseur (*slang*)	gear (*slang*)	bleach	discerning
horn-rimmed (spectacles)	stretch to	painstakingly	lanky	slashing	
gratifying	to sport	tails (tail coat)	darned	patched	

15

CHIC OR FREAK?

The distress of the young began in the 1970's and despite all the efforts of teachers and parents, it has refused to go away. This has nothing to do with psychological or physical disorders, it isn't caused by unemployment, and it is not caused by concern at the sorry state of the world: it is the distressed *look*.

Take Jan, for instance. When he was seventeen, he was tall and lanky, wore red-rimmed spectacles and shortish hair. The casual poseur mode was already part of his past, and he looked back with shame on that time so long before – was it six months? – when every sweater had to bear a little green crocodile emblem if he was not to be refused entry to decent homes.

Now his only concession to casual gear was his pair of white leather baseball boots. Now he was no longer casual but pre-distressed. Every newly-purchased item in his wardrobe had to be savagely attacked and rendered totally harmless. He bought in cans of industrial bleach to give that washed-out look to his jeans and shirts, and occasional streaks of hair. He was a discerning purchaser of razor blades, not for his hairless chin, but for slashing blue denim. Jeans fresh from the shop were knelt in until gratifying holes appeared at the knees. Hems of shirts and jeans were unpicked and painstakingly frayed. His one ear-ring was a paper clip.

His ear-lobe for a time was also distressed – it started to fray where it had been pierced. The holes in the jeans became a little inconvenient when the winter winds started to blow, and as a great concession to comfort, it was permissible to wear tights underneath – as long as they were, say, red, or black and were not intended to disguise the existence of the prestigious holes.

Two years on, now that he is nineteen, he is still tall and lanky, but his range of distress has expanded to take in other styles. His glasses are horn-rimmed and his hair is strictly short-back-and-sides. On the upper part of his body he sports a white shirt with a separate butterfly wing collar and occasionally a white evening waistcoat. He prefers to wear a dinner jacket, though he has been known to stretch to a full set of tails. He wears a black tie or no tie at all. His jeans are still frayed, but the holes are now darned or patched, with red wool or tartan patches. The distressed look is still essential. On his feet he still wears his now decreasingly casual and increasingly distressed white baseball boots.

Check your understanding

1. For what purpose were the following items bought?
   bleach razors paper clips
2. What process did new jeans and shirts have to undergo to make them look acceptable?
3. In order to be allowed into respectable homes, Jan once had to . . .
   - **a** wear a green crocodile with his sweaters.
   - **b** be casually but smartly dressed.
   - **c** be tall and lanky.
4. How has Jan's style altered over the space of two years?
5. Is there anything odd about his clothes now?
6. Describe a 'butterfly-wing' collar.

Group discussion

- Is this an invented figure? Does anyone you know really dress like this? What items of clothing described above would you like to wear and what would you not want to wear?
- Would you like your boyfriend or girlfriend to look like this? Why? Why not?
- In what ways do you think teenage fashions will change in the next two years?
- Young people in your country may like to dress distinctively but not in the way described above. In what distinctive way do they dress?

GRAMMAR GUIDE

Verbs which take the gerund

'This seems simpler, cheaper and would avoid their getting lost . . .'

When one verb follows another, the second is not always in the infinitive. In the example, *avoid* is followed by the *-ing* form of *get*.

Avoid is usually followed by the *-ing* form. A number of other verbs behave in the same way. The commonest include:

admit	involve	give up	practise
appreciate	enjoy	can't help	resist
consider	escape	understand	risk
delay	face	mention	can't stand
detest	feel like	mind	suggest
dislike	finish		

Make sure you understand the meanings of the verbs above.

Practice

Complete these sentences in your own way, using gerunds.

eg The thief admitted ____________________ .

1 I really don't feel like ____________________ .

2 She has never mentioned ____________________ .

3 Mountain climbers always risk ____________________ .

4 Being a member of a team involves ____________________ .

5 I have written to ask if she would consider ____________________ .

6 People used to enjoy ____________________ .

7 After an all-night party I can't face ____________________ .

8 You're getting fat, you've got to give up ____________________ .

9 Her voice is so loud I can't stand ____________________ .

10 The food is so bad at our house that guests really dislike ____________________ .

Now make five more sentences of your own.

Sentence transformation

Re-write the sentences below, using the new word but keeping the meaning.

eg A number of people have complained about the mistreatment of animals. (*complaints*)
A number of people have made complaints about the mistreatment of animals.

Animals can become more aggressive if they are provoked. (*aggression*)

We should not give way to self-congratulation. (*congratulate*)

The viewing public makes allegations about biased reports on TV. (*alleges*)

My friends and I celebrated at the pub. (*celebration*)

It is one of the few studies to make a confident connection between television and violence. (*connect*)

The authorities ought to forbid the showing of such films. (*a ban*)

Cave art has its origins in the superstitions of ancient tribes. (*originates*)

Vocabulary

The following is a letter written by a soldier in 1944. The military censor has blanked out any references in the letter which might give the enemy a clue to where the soldier is. Try to reconstruct the original letter. The words and phrases at the end may help you.

Somewhere in England
... June 1944

Dear Mum,
So this is it! ▬▬▬ we set off for the great invasion we have been waiting for for so long. ▬▬▬ was my ▬▬▬ and I celebrated with my comrades in a pub at ▬▬▬ which is ▬▬▬ from here, ▬▬▬ It was a ▬▬▬ walk back, I can tell you! We have been issued with lots of ▬▬▬ equipment for when we ▬▬▬ on the ▬▬▬ in ▬▬▬ We don't know where it will be yet. Or when. It all depends on the ▬▬▬, and it might be put off again. The whole place is swarming with ▬▬▬ and ▬▬▬ I'm glad we haven't been issued with ▬▬▬ . That certainly means we will be going over in ▬▬▬. All the ▬▬▬ are jammed full of ▬▬▬ ▬▬▬ but I don't like them at all, I get so ▬▬▬
Lot's of love, I'll write again from Over There!

Your son

airfields
due south
weather
Canadians
Tomorrow
ten miles
wooden gliders
long
beaches
Poles
birthday
airsick
boats
mine-clearing
France
parachutes
Ditchling
land
Yesterday

DIARY pp. 58–61

Day(s) Date(s) Month Year

Texts

OK

Look at again

Ask the teacher

Look up in reference books

To remember

New Words

Grammar

Useful phrases

Unit 16

WHERE SPORT MEETS POLITICS

discussion

Who are these people?
Which countries are they from?
Which sports are they associated with?

What do you think is special about each of them?

Now meet Nawal El Moutawakel, the first Arab woman – the first African woman – to win an Olympic gold medal.

Reading

A moment of history

Let us recall an historic event that occurred only recently. In August 1984, at the Los Angeles Olympic Games, a young Moroccan woman, Nawal El Moutawakel, won the first gold medal ever to be awarded to an Arab woman. "For an Arab woman, winning is really something!" she exclaimed.

The Coliseum held its breath and shed a tear. On the running track, a slip of a girl in a green vest reeled with happiness, leaning forward with her hands on her knees as if the whole weight of the world had suddenly fallen onto her narrow shoulders.

The significance of the occasion was not lost on the Coliseum; it knew that it was experiencing a rare moment. Later, it learned that Nawal El Moutawakel, not content with winning the 400 m hurdles, had just picked up Morocco's first ever gold medal and become the first African woman to achieve that incomparable status.

That Wednesday, the young Moroccan not only won a race; she performed a feat likely to spark off a mini-revolution in a continent that had previously been unaccustomed to seeing a woman take such initiatives.

Readers will no doubt remember when African athletes first burst onto the sporting scene, arousing both admiration and hope. When Abebe Bikila won a gold medal in the marathon in 1960, when Wilson Kiprugut improved the Olympic 800 m record in 1964, when Kipchoge Keino beat the 3 000 m world record in 1965, the whole of Africa took inspiration from these events and the world was provided with evidence of the continent's inexhaustible resources.

Over and above its joyous reaction to these athletic feats, a whole continent demanded the right to ambition and announced its desire to advance itself. Despite the handicaps inherent in chronic under-development and under-equipment, the Kenyan, Ugandan, Ethiopian, Tanzanian and Nigerian athletes have gradually asserted themselves at the highest level, reaping their harvest of medals after each Olympic Games.

Until that Wednesday, women, labouring under social and religious pressures, had been entirely excluded from this general movement. Even though Nawal El Moutawakel's feat was achieved in a race appearing in the Olympic programme for the first time, and in the absence of the Soviets who are usually highly effective in that area, it marked the starting point of a fresh conquest. Not surprisingly, that 22-year-old girl came from a country where sport enjoys special consideration. Morocco, which hosted the Mediterranean Games in 1983, has discovered a new vocation.

Check your understanding

Who or what . . .

eg held its breath?:

Answer The Coliseum (at the Los Angeles Olympic Games, 1984).

1 shed a tear?
2 reeled with happiness?
3 was not lost on the Coliseum?
4 knew that it was experiencing a rare moment?
5 won a gold medal in the 1960 marathon?
6 took inspiration from these events (Olympic victories)?
7 was provided with evidence of the continent's (Africa's) inexhaustible resources?
8 demanded the right to ambition and announced its desire to advance itself?
9 marked the starting point of a fresh conquest?
10 hosted the Mediterranean games in 1983?

Listening

Listen to the passage from 'Radio Sports Magazine' which takes a look at sport and politics from an historical angle. Make notes while you are listening and then answer the questions.

Before listening, check the meaning of the words below.

thud	serialise	public school
fixation	incredulous	resurrect
allay	counterpart	discomfiture
ostentatious	overburden	

Answer these questions.

1 What would you expect a comic to contain?
   a romantic stories told in pictures
   b funny cartoon stories
   c adventure serials
2 Orwell discovered that comics were read mainly by children of the very rich. True or false?
3 What were comic stories mainly concerned with?
4 How were sports stories often presented?
5 What other obsession did sports writers have?
6 Explain the meaning of the term 'Great White Hope'.
7 In what way were British youngsters made to feel inferior to African youth?
8 Why did the comic book stories produce white super-champions?
9 What was the reality of the world of boxing and athletics?
10 Jesse Owens is remembered for two things at the 1936 Olympics. What were they?
11 How many years has it taken the world to realise that the success of non-white athletes has had little bearing on politics?
12 What significance does the sporting triumph of Third World athletes really have?

Project

Prepare a short talk on a famous sports personality from your country. Divide your presentation into three parts:

Personal details	name, sex, age, important dates, family, education
Sporting achievements	which sport, records and medals
Influences	on sport itself, your country's reputation

Remember to make notes about your friends' talks. You will need these notes later!

GRAMMAR GUIDE

The passive: infinitive, present simple, past simple

1 INFINITIVE

> *to award* (something) = infinitive (active voice)
> *to be awarded* = infinitive (passive voice)

eg Nawal El Moutawakel's Olympic gold medal was the first to be awarded to an Arab woman.

Practice

1 Change these active infinitives into passive infinitives.
eg to admire ⇒ to be admired

to forget	to open	to take
to give	to order	to use
to forgive	to remove	to win
to love		

2 Complete each of the following with the correct passive infinitive, using verbs from the previous exercise.

eg ____________ three times a day	Not ____________ until Christmas Day!
Bingo tonight! Lots of prizes ____________	____________ only in cases of emergency
Mum's birthday! Definitely NOT ____________!	Chef's special Lobster Thermidor ____________ at least one day in advance

2 PRESENT SIMPLE

> Football *is watched* by millions of people, but it *isn't liked* by everybody.
> The Olympics *are organised* every four years, but they *aren't held* in the same place every time.

Practice

Ask and answer questions about sport in your school/town/country. Reply with any appropriate verb, using the present simple passive, affirmative or negative.

1 Do many people play sport?
2 Do a lot of people watch tennis?
3 Do people admire sports personalities?
4 Does anyone organise local competitions?
5 Does the radio broadcast sport a lot?
6 Do people know about cricket?
7 Which age group plays . . . most?
8 On which days does TV show most sport?
9 How do the newspapers treat . . .?
10 Do a lot of people attend . . .?

3 PAST SIMPLE

'Julius Caesar' *was written* by Shakespeare – it *wasn't written* by Charles Dickens!
In Shakespeare's day, his plays *were performed* by men only. They *weren't acted* by women until some time later.

Practice

Correct these statements. Say *No, he/she/it wasn't! He/she/it was . . . No, they weren't! They were . . .*

1 John F. Kennedy was assassinated in New York.
2 The James Bond novels were written by Sean Connery.
3 The hydrogen bomb was invented by the Russians.
4 Mount Everest was first conquered by the Chinese.
5 The Beatles' first records were made in the USA.
6 The British Isles were last invaded in 1588.
7 The 'Choral Symphony' was composed by Mozart.
8 The first atom bomb was dropped on Nagasaki.
9 The Olympic Games were originally held in ancient Rome.
10 Originally, records were played at 87 revolutions per minute.

Vocabulary practice

Each word on the ladder is from the reading text. Complete the ladder by adding other appropriate words in the same categories.

gold					successes
silver	exclaim				
bronze		marathon	highest	years	

Now see who can extend the ladder the most. Take any two or three ladders, and add as many appropriate words – in the right order – as you can!

Writing

1 In small groups, discuss the proposition that sport cannot be separated from politics, then write a short essay on the same topic in not more than 400 words.

2 Look at the notes you made on your friend's talk (see page 63). Use them to write a short composition about the sports personality chosen by your friend.

DIARY			pp. 62–65
Day(s)	Date(s)	Month	Year
Texts		**To remember**	
OK		New Words	
Look at again			
Ask the teacher		Grammar	
Look up in reference books		Useful phrases	

Unit 17
IT'S A MAN'S WORLD

Group discussion

Throughout the world cooking in the home is mostly done by women, and yet professional cooks and chefs are more often men.

Can you think of any reasons why this should be the case? Could it be that women can't stand the heat, or perhaps they feel less than feminine in a chef's uniform? Might the anti-social working hours be off-putting, or do they simply not want to leave work every day smelling of fried onions? What do you think?

Reading

A Professional Chef

Anton is a teacher of cookery at a college in Darwin in Australia. He has his own radio show as well. He is this month's guest interviewed by the catering journal *End Cuts*.

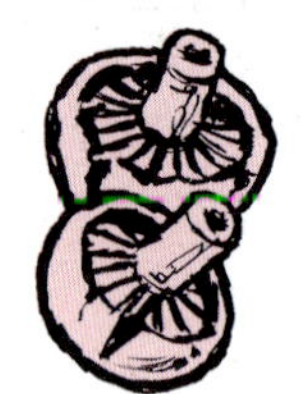

I was born in Austria. After leaving school at the age of sixteen I attended a 'pudding school' in Vienna, and picked up various qualifications as a chef. I worked for some years in the hotel business but the travel bug bit me and I emigrated to Melbourne in Australia.

I had quite a hard time of it there at first, slogging away for all kinds of hours in all kinds of restaurants, earning very little – though I never had to go hungry!

My main survival problem was getting my English up to scratch. While I became very adept at talking to fellow chefs, kitchen staff and customers and I had a good command of colloquial and even abusive language, I was only too aware that my English had yawning gaps in it. I tried to attend day classes at a local migrant college whenever I could.

After a few years, an international chain advertised a job in a hotel on a tourist island in the South Pacific. I applied, went for interview and got the job. Officially my title was 'sous-chef' but in fact when I was on duty I had to shoulder the whole responsibility for keeping the hotel restaurant going: ordering supplies, planning weekly and daily menus, hiring kitchen staff, assigning work, and when it came down to it, doing some cooking myself.

It was sometimes pleasant work, but it was very demanding and the heat of the kitchen was mostly unimaginable. I had my moments of triumph, such as the time when a waiter skidded disastrously and dropped a magnificent iced cake I had made specially for a party of guests celebrating a birthday. I clapped my hands, the doors opened again and a second waiter glided through carrying another cake which I had made as a back-up. (I had once read about this happening to the chef at Maxim's in Paris at the turn of the century and on special occasions tried it myself. I only needed to produce the spare cake on this one occasion, though.)

When my three-year contract ended I decided to try my hand in London. While looking for a job I stayed with some friends – for rather a long time, as it turned out, because I didn't have much luck.

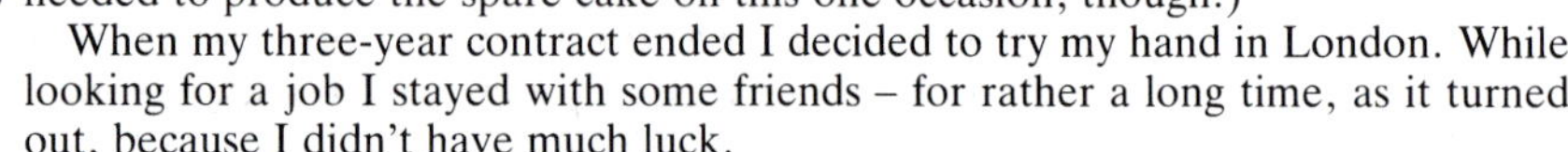

After that I worked for a year in Sri Lanka and then went back to Melbourne. I spent about two years there and them moved up to Darwin – got this lecturing job – and here I am!

Check your understanding

1 Are these statements correct? If not, explain why.

- **a** Anton realised he had to do something about the quality of his English.
- **b** Anton is a native Australian.
- **c** He made a cake the same as one served at Maxim's in Paris.
- **d** 'Sous chef' was an inadequate description of his job in the South Pacific.
- **e** His friends helped him look for a job.

2 Search the text for ideas to begin these sentences. Use your own words.

- **a** ______________________ while I tried unsuccessfully to find work.
- **b** ______________________ but I spent many years in the hotel and catering industry.
- **c** ______________________ but the title was hardly accurate.
- **d** ______________________ because I wanted to see some of the rest of the world.
- **e** ______________________ because of an incident I'd read about.

3 Find words or phrases in the text which mean the same as these:

College of Catering	working hard	I wanted to travel
gained qualifications	improve my language	my English lacked something

Listening

This is a recorded interview with Leslie Woodstock, a semi-professional house-husband.

Before you listen, look up these words:

a croupier	archaeological dig
pocket money	fluffy
obsessive	genes
gadget	yolk

While you listen . . .

There are some things in what he said that might make you think Leslie Woodstock is not entirely truthful about his positive attitude to working at home. Listen to the interview again and note down any expressions which might make you doubtful. You will need these later.

Check your understanding

1 Choose the correct word/phrase to complete these sentences:

Leslie's wife works in a ______________________.
a night time **b** casino **c** laundry

Leslie ______________________ to doing most housework jobs.
a has no objection **b** objects **c** refuses

Leslie's wife is ______________________ fussy than he is.
a less **b** more **c** just as

Leslie enjoys ______________________ more than any other activity.
a washing **b** shopping **c** cooking

In the Woodstock house, the real cleaning is done ______________________ .
a every year **b** during a storm **c** at holiday times

17 GRAMMAR GUIDE

Present simple narrative

The Present Simple tense can be used to refer to things that happen regularly, to refer to the future, to make commentaries on sporting events, and to tell stories which happened in the past. It is often used to create atmosphere.
Listen to the Woodstock interview again. Make a note of which parts are told in the Present Simple. Work with a partner and compare notes. How does Leslie use the Present Simple? Think of five sentences about yourself using the Present Simple the same way as Leslie does. Write them down.

Practice

Expand the following ideas into a story and tell it in the Present Simple Narrative. (You might like to record it and add some sound effects!)

Fog rises – night time – quayside.

Ship's horn – melancholy wail.

Cat burglar – in shadows – victim – front door of house.

Leaves.

Burglar – up drainpipe – balcony.

Window – steps inside. Victim returns.

Scream – a shot – silence.

Shadowy figure – front door.

Distance – police siren – silent again.

Present simple commentary

Choose the right verbs from the list below and put them in the Present Simple form to fill the gaps:

place	gather	hurl	push	move	wait	tap	dribble	flip	smash
do not	swerve	let							

At the beginning of the second half it is the UEFA side to kick off. Beckenbauer ________ the ball on the spot and ________ for the referee to blow his whistle. He ________ it back to Stanley Matthews who ________ it forward into the other half before lobbing it over to Pucskas, who ________ over onto his back and ________ it left-footed over his head at the goalkeeper. But Frank Swift, dependable as ever ________ it in his huge hands and ________ it far into the opponent's side, right to the feet of Pele, who is immediately brought down in a sliding tackle to his shins by Tommy Lawton. Free kick. The referee ________ the wall of defenders back. I can see Charlton there, Tommy Doherty, Maradona, all jockeying to block the line of sight to goalkeeper Yashin. Muller ________ forward to take the shot, no he ________, he ________ to the left and ________ Dixie Dean curl it round the wall and into the arms of Yashin. Goal kick.

Role play

Work with a partner:

You are the Marketing Director for a company which makes very fashionable clothes. Your assistant is going on a round-the-world sales trip that you have planned. Decide the route, then give your assistant an outline of the plans, eg 'On Monday 17 April, you leave London Airport at 0600 hrs and take an Air Global flight to Helsinki . . .'

Marketing Assistant: You are not happy with the plans. Challenge them, suggest alternatives, but try not to upset the boss too much. You don't want to lose your job!

Vocabulary practice

The following sentences each have a word or words missing. Choose the correct one to complete each sentence:

It is often difficult to plan a household ______________
(*account budget finance money*)

In England, ______________ was traditionally done on Mondays.
(*clothing washing-up the washing launderette*)

I wish we had a dish-washer. I'm tired of this endless ______________
(*pots and pans hand-washing dirty dishes washing-up*)

Can you do ______________ after you've had lunch?
(*the shopping shops the buying shopping*)

We need more ______________ in this wardrobe.
(*coat hooks clothes line coat hangers places*)

Can you iron the ______________ out of this shirt, please?
(*dents lines folds creases*)

Have you a twenty pence ______________ to pay the car park attendant?
(*money change coin silver*)

DIARY pp. 66–69

Day(s) Date(s) Month Year

Texts

OK

Look at again

Ask the teacher

Look up in reference books

To remember

New Words

Grammar

Useful phrases

Unit 18

YOU ARE WHAT YOU EAT

This unit could also be called 'Food Concern' – concern about possibly unwelcome additives to our food. It also brings to your attention a rather bizarre new addition to our gourmet diet.

Group project

Visit your local supermarket and check the labels on a selection of branded goods. Make a list of the foods and the additives they contain. These may be coded with the letter E and a number. Having drawn up your list, try to find out what the codes stand for and present your findings to the class.

Ingredients

DRIED GLUCLOSE SYRUP, MODIFIED STARCH, VEGETABLE FAT, SALT, FLAVOUR ENHANCER (621), DRIED MUSHROOMS, HYDROLYSED VEGETABLE PROTEIN, STABILISER (E412), ONION POWDER, CASEINATE, ACIDITY REGULATOR (E340), EMULSIFIERS (E471, E472e), COLOURS (E150, E171) HERBS & SPICES, FLAVOURINGS, ARTIFICIAL SWEETENER (SACCHARIN)

Reading

Before reading, check the meanings of the following words and phrases:

culinary	herds	look-alike	fad
substitute	ball bearings	revolting	phased out
palate	canapé	trail of slime	flash in the pan
textured vegetable protein	gourmet market	the last word	

Caviar Français

In the old days, twenty or so years ago, eating in Moscow was a lesser culinary delight. Restaurants were few and far between and more often than not the poor tourist found himself in a *stolovaya*, or public dining room, where all the meals were the same – you got meatballs and gravy for breakfast, lunch and dinner. Any time of the day or night you got meatballs. Mind you, you also got caviar – both the black kind from the sturgeon, looking like ball bearings in machine oil, and more usually the big red kind from the salmon. But with the increasing pollution of the Volga and the Caspian Sea, where the sturgeon was at home, and with over-fishing, caviar is becoming a rarer commodity and is no longer served for breakfast.

Obviously the search for a substitute is on. Refined canapé palates cannot accept the cheaper lumpfish caviar look-alikes (but not taste-alikes) and, until caviar can be manufactured out of textured vegetable protein, caviar farming is on the cards. The latest delicacy to come on to the French gourmet market is snail caviar, or 'caviar français' as it is known.

And why not, one asks. Snails themselves are a great delicacy, and so why should one not regard their eggs in the same way? The eggs are large, about the size of salmon eggs, but they are white and when eaten each grain gives a satisfying pop in the mouth, as good caviar should. The idea was developed by Alain Chatillon, a French 'philosopher' and 'treasure hunter', as he prefers to call himself.

He found this particular treasure while on a visit to a temple in Tibet. Seeing small cups filled with snails' eggs placed as offerings before statues of the deity, instead of shuddering as one might expect, Chatillon dipped his finger in and quickly tasted the eggs. 'They were quite revolting', he said later. These eggs are regarded in Tibet as symbols of everlasting life.

Back home in the Languedoc in France, he set about finding a variety which is not quite so disgusting, and he now claims to have succeeded. But at 6000 francs a kilo, the caviar français produced from 'herds' of snails on snail ranches is no cheaper than the real thing from the sturgeon. The smell which is rather like that of marzipan suggests that they are sweet, but in fact they taste salty. Each snail on the farm lays some 3.5 grams of eggs, compared with each sturgeon's 20 kilos, which means that it takes 5700 snails to compete with a sturgeon, but the economics must be right, for snail caviar farming is catching on.

The problem essentially is not what the eggs taste like but of overcoming the psychological barrier to eating the products of creatures that leave a trail of slime on the garden path and which one knows to be hermaphrodite – both male and female at the same time. However, this resistance is breaking down and caviar français is fast becoming the last word in gourmet restaurants up and down the country.

Now answer the questions.

1. What could one expect to eat in a *stolovaya*?
2. Name two fish that produce caviar.
3. Why is it necessary to search for a caviar substitute?
4. Describe the difference between snail and sturgeon caviar.
5. Where did Chatillon get the idea for snail caviar?
6. What does it cost per kilo?
7. What consumer problem still needs to be overcome and why?
8. Why does the writer describe Moscow as 'a lesser culinary delight' (line 2)?
9. What does the author mean when he says caviar looks like 'ball bearings in machine oil' (line 9)?
10. Explain 'snail caviar farming is catching on' (line 48).

Group discussion

Divide into small groups. Make a list of all the foods which you regard as especially revolting. Come together afterwards and compare lists. Draw up a list of the ten most disliked foods. (These must be real foods, not imaginary ones.) Are there any reasons for the general dislike of these foods? Try to find out.

Listening

The listening passage is an extract from the 'Healthy Eating Programme', which has been looking into public concern about food additives. As you listen, write down any new words and find out what they mean.

Take notes while listening and answer the following questions.

1. Why are manufacturers being pressed to remove all artificial colourings from their products?
2. To what does the Ocean Wave Company attribute its success?
3. What quantity of artificial colouring is consumed annually in Britain?
4. Why have Sureways Supermarkets taken steps to remove food additives from their goods?
5. What colour do we expect smoked haddock to be?
6. Why is the public becoming hostile to glamorised food?

Project

Do you object to food additives? If you do, what steps could you take to ensure their removal?

Think about the formation of a pressure group, how you could get your message across to the maximum number of people for the minimum cost, how you could convince people to give you their active support. Plan a campaign!

The passive: perfect

The Passive Perfect is used when we wish to emphasise the grammatical subject of the sentence at the expense of the agent.

eg The idea of snail caviar has been developed by Alain Chatillon.

It is also used when the agent is unknown or unimportant.

eg Snail eggs have been used as offerings to gods in Tibetan temples for centuries.

Changing active into passive sentences

That boy has broken the window again.

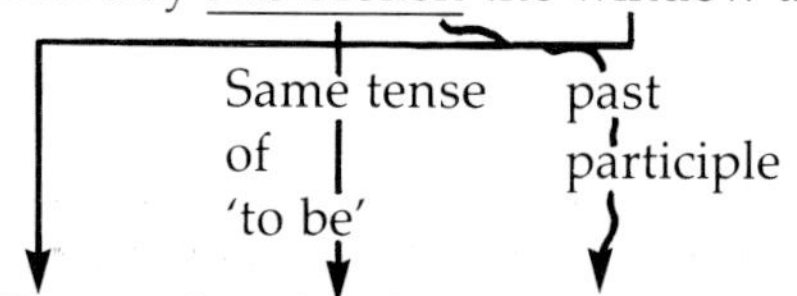

The window has been broken again (by that boy).

(**Note** that we do not have to mention the 'agent', ie who was responsible for the action, unless we think it is important.)

Practice

1 Change these sentences about the text from the active to the passive, as in the example.
eg They have not served caviar for breakfast for some time in the Russian *stolovaya*.
⇒ Caviar has not been served for breakfast in the Russian stolovaya for some time

- **a** Recently restaurateurs have demanded a substitute for caviar.
- **b** Gourmets have always regarded snails as a great delicacy.
- **c** Alain Chatillon has spent a great deal of time developing caviar.
- **d** Chatillon has improved the taste and quality of his snail caviar.

2 Change the following sentences into the past or the perfect form of the passive.

- **a** You haven't cooked these potatoes.
- **b** They threw away all the old furniture.
- **c** He didn't repair the clock.
- **d** The local women's group have organised the exhibition.
- **e** Someone called Thatcher stole our car.
- **f** A palace spokesman read out the announcement.
- **g** Some friends have redecorated my flat.
- **h** Only one person read the report.

Pair work

Work with a partner. Using the words suggested, make questions and then answer them in the Passive Perfect, as in the example.

eg Eat/lot/vegetables/rice
Q Have people always eaten a lot of vegetables in your country?
A Quite a lot, but I think rice has been eaten even more.

1 read/weekly newspapers/daily newspapers
2 live in/flats/houses
3 eat/convenience food/home-cooked food
4 drink/tea/coffee
5 wear/fashionable shoes/comfortable shoes
6 play/baseball/soccer

Check your prepositions!

The prepositions have been removed from the following paragraph. Fill each of the blanks with a suitable preposition to complete the text.

Chatillon was ________ holiday in Tibet when he came ________ a temple high ________ the Himalayas which had been built ________ a group of Tibetans who belonged ________ an obscure religious order. They put him ________ for a few days. He was free to wander ________ the place ________ any time of the day or night and could join ________ their ceremonies as he wished. It was ________ one such occasion that Chatillon discovered snails' eggs that might be worth developing ________ a commercial enterprise.

Been + gone

These words are often confused.

We use *gone* if someone is either on his way to a place or is actually there now.

eg Jan has gone to Oxford and won't be back until Sunday.

We use *been* if someone has travelled to a place and come back again.

eg She's been to Paris twice this year.
Have you ever been to Finland?

Been is also used with the meaning of come and gone away again.

eg They've been to see us quite a lot lately.

Practice

Complete the following sentences with either *been* or *gone*.

1 I've already ________ to France. Let's try Italy this time.
2 They've all ________ to the cinema. I'm staying in to do my hair.
3 I've ________ everywhere looking for Jack and now I find he's ________ to the coast. He's not due back for a week.
4 Sarah's ________ abroad twice this year. Martha's ________ to Manchester for a short break and gets back tomorrow and that leaves Alice who's never ________ anywhere!
5 Don't tell me where you've ________, I don't want to know, but one day you'll find that I've ________ and won't be back!

DIARY pp. 70–73

Day(s)	Date(s)	Month	Year

Texts	**To remember**
OK	New Words
Look at again	
Ask the teacher	Grammar
Look up in reference books	Useful phrases

19

Unit 19

NEW FORMS OF NUCLEAR THREAT

The Chernobyl accident has awakened fears that nuclear disaster may come not from the results of an exchange of missiles but from the so-called 'peaceful' uses of atomic energy.

Listening

Dilys is a teacher who is a member of CND. While you listen to her, make notes under the headings below.

Reasons for joining	Activities national and local	Disarmament

Group discussion

Working in small groups, discuss how you as a group could exist after a nuclear catastrophe, with no houses, no fresh water or food, no sources of power (electricity or gas), no medical aid, no transport, temperatures are very low and at least half the group has been very badly injured.

Tell the other groups your ideas and then decide as a class which plans present the greatest possibilities for your survival.

Reading

Before reading, check the meaning of the following words and phrases:

plume	predicted	abortive	accident-prone	spill	manned by	precaution
fanciful	deplete	contaminates	uninhabitable	collision	molten	eventuality

Ever since the first atomic bombs were dropped on Hiroshima and Nagasaki, governments have been at pains to stress that the atom has a peaceful as well as a warlike side. In early propaganda films to win the populace round to the idea of a nuclear research program, we were shown pictures of a high speed train travelling around the world, powered, so the commentator said, by the equivalent of the energy contained in a glass of water. Energy won by 'harnessing the power of the atom', it was claimed, would be cheap, efficient, clean, and above all safe. No longer, it was said, would men have to labour beneath the ground in dirty and dangerous conditions to win the coal which would fuel our industry. The nuclear power stations of the future, we were told, since they did not depend on burning fossil fuels like coal or oil, would not deplete the world's natural resources and hence were a good thing.

It all took a lot longer to happen than predicted. The first disappointment, of course, was that they could not actually fuel a power station with a glass of water. Early experiments suggesting that this would be possible proved abortive. No, the power stations still had to be fuelled with radioactive and potentially dangerous substances won, like coal, from the ground by accident-prone miners. These substances had to be transported to the power stations by train in special containers. Many of the early objections and protest campaigns came from the inhabitants of villages through which such trains passed, who feared that in the event of a collision the containers of radioactive substances would break and spill radiation on to surrounding houses and countryside. The railway authorities were fairly successful in allaying such fears and showing that the containers they used could never break, not even in a head-on collision.

Concern was almost never directed at the power stations themselves, which, we were assured by confident voices, were manned by scientists in white coats who had taken every precaution and foreseen every eventuality. What the nuclear power station designers and engineers had not taken into account, however, was Murphy's Law which states that if a thing can possibly go wrong, sooner or later it will. And so it proved at Three Mile Island in the USA, and Windscale in the UK. Accidents were happening despite all precautions, radiation was spilling into the atmosphere and we heard for the first time of the China Syndrome – the dreadful possibility of a nuclear accident burning through the earth all the way to China.

This was dismissed as a fanciful concept until Chernobyl, the world's worst nuclear accident so far. We saw pictures of a 'melt-down', where the entire core of the reactor becomes molten and uncontrollable, but also heard for the first time of a 'melt-through', where the radioactive mass melts through the earth's crust and at the very least contaminates the ground water of an entire river basin system, rendering thousands of square miles uninhabitable for decades and totally destroying the agriculture of an entire region.

The fact that it was not quite as catastrophic as this is due to the incredible and heroic self-sacrifice of Soviet fire-fighters who tunnelled beneath the molten mass, entering the radioactive zone, to build a shield of concrete beneath the power station and wall it off for ever. In the meantime the plume of radioactivity had risen high above western Europe and, with the rain, dropped, deadeningly in Sweden.

Europe and the world were faced with an ecological disaster as great as any posed by an accidental firing of a military weapon, and suddenly, without a shot being fired in anger, the 'peaceful uses of atomic energy' did not seem so peaceful any more.

Check your understanding

1 Explain the meaning of these words and phrases as they are used in the text:
fossil fuels allay fears Earth's crust wall it off

2 Replace the following words and phrases with an explanation in your own words:
governments have been at pains to stress harnessing the power of the atom
natural resources won from the ground melt-down ecological disaster

3 Are the following statements true or false?

- a People have reason to fear more than one kind of nuclear disaster.
- b Claims were made that nuclear power would present no danger.
- c Both nuclear and fossil fuels have to be mined.
- d People have stopped objecting to the transportation of nuclear fuels by rail.
- e Scientists had anticipated every possible problem with nuclear reactors.
- f The potential effects of the Chernobyl disaster could have been just as bad as the explosion of a nuclear weapon.

Project

Divide into small groups. Each group is to choose one of the following topics:

- Cruise missiles
- Star Wars defence
- Nuclear waste disposal
- Alternative non-nuclear defence weapons
- Civil Defence and nuclear bunkers
- Anti-nuclear pressure groups

Find out as much as you can about your chosen topic.
How? Contact your local/national branch of CND or your local Civil Defence organisation.
Go to the local library. Look in the Reference Section.
Scan newspapers or magazines, particularly international or scientific ones.

Prepare a short talk. Begin with the more general information then follow with specific details. Mention the sources of the information. Illustrate the presentation with pictures, charts or anything you think may be of interest.

19 GRAMMAR GUIDE

Conditional 2

IF + PAST TENSE	+	WOULD/SHOULD MAY/MIGHT COULD

These conditionals are often called clauses of hypothetical condition. The condition is one that is thought to be impossible or contrary to fact or unlikely to happen or which has not yet happened.
eg If a bomb exploded we might survive for a while.

Practice

1 Expand the following into sentences using the Conditional 2 pattern.

- **a** If governments began to be more conscientious . . .
- **b** People would be in great danger . . .
- **c** If everyone built fallout shelters . . .
- **d** If we were given the ten-minute warning . . .
- **e** Nothing as we know it would continue to exist . . .
- **f** If those opposed to all nuclear weapons protested . . .
- **g** If unilateral disarmament were to be achieved . . .
- **h** It is possible that a treaty could be agreed . . .

> 'If' can sometimes be replaced by 'Suppose/Supposing' in Conditional 2 questions. The meaning is the same but the style is less formal.

eg {Suppose / Supposing} he asked you to work with him, what would you say?

2 Now make beginnings for these questions starting with 'Suppose/Supposing'.

- **a** . . . what could they do?
- **b** . . . how would they spend it?
- **c** . . . where would we go?
- **d** . . . why should he tell us?
- **e** . . . when could we do something about it?

Vocabulary practice

The verbs in brackets are apparently identical in meaning. But in the sentences below only one is correct. Choose the right one.

1 The church bells {aroused / stimulated} us from our beds.

2 The uranium was {achieved / won} at great cost from the mountain.

3 The Volga {spilled over / overflowed} its banks again this year.

4 The politician {dismissed / sacked} the reports as outrageous.

5 After 60 years service the company {gave / presented} its employees with a gold watch.

6 The holidaymakers were allowed to {pick / choose} twelve pounds of strawberries from the field.

Word sets

Look at the words below which are all connected in some way with atomic energy. Place them in the appropriate box according to whether they have positive, negative or neutral connotations.

accident	energy	peaceful	power
survival	research	electricity	awakened fears
atom	cheap	contaminates	scientists
efficient	reactor	clean	safe
dangerous	melt-down	uncontrollable	warlike
shield	uninhabitable	heroic	self-sacrifice
catastrophic	radioactive	ecological	white coats

1 NEUTRAL	2 NEGATIVE	3 POSITIVE

Write two short paragraphs about the negative and positive sides of atomic energy, using the words from boxes 2 and 3.

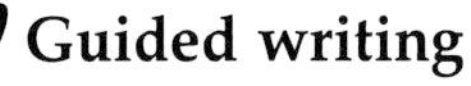

Guided writing

Fill out these headlines into a continuous account in the past tense of the Chernobyl disaster.

RADIOACTIVE CLOUD MEASURED OVER EUROPE

UKRAINE EVACUATION BEGINS

US spy satellite films glow at Soviet power station

Engineers mine under danger zone

POLLUTION OF UKRAINIAN RIVER SYSTEM FEARED

World concern at Chernobyl danger

SOVIETS ADMIT NUCLEAR ACCIDENT

RUSSIANS SEAL OFF CHERNOBYL IN CONCRETE TOMB

SOVIETS PLAY DOWN MELT-THROUGH FEARS

Can it happen elsewhere? asks anxious world

DIARY pp. 74–77

Day(s) Date(s) Month Year

Texts

OK

Look at again

Ask the teacher

Look up in reference books

To remember

New Words

Grammar

Useful phrases

Unit 20

FAMINE
a political issue

In 1985 and 1986 one man, Bob Geldof, an unshaven, unkempt Irish rock musician came to personify the conscience of the thinking West toward the terrible famine sweeping Africa.

Opening discussion

Look at the list of food items below. Divide them into two groups, those which you consider essential and non-essential respectively. Is there anything else that you feel ought to be added to the list of essentials?

rice	salt	cheese
fish	milk	green cabbage
bread	apples	beef
oil	honey	spaghetti
lamb chops	beans	butter
carrots	prawns	jam
chips	bacon	cake
hamburger	eggs	tomatoes
chocolate	bananas	sugar

If you had to choose only four foods from your list of essentials, which would you select? Consult other students. Try to agree on the four items chosen. Convince the others if you feel very strongly about something

Reading

Before reading, check the meaning of these words:

to spawn	hyperbole	candour	halo	hailed	steadfastly	exuberance	ensnare

Not long ago Bob Geldof was just a rock musician. His group, the Boomtown Rats, was on the slide. But then he assembled forty rock stars to record a song he helped to write to raise money for famine relief in Ethiopia. Few would have predicted that *Do They Know It's Christmas?* would become the fastest-selling single in British pop history and raise £8m; fewer still predicted that it would spawn two massively successful Live Aid concerts which would raise a further £50m. In fact, by the end of 1985 people everywhere were pressing money into Geldof's hand, and he was being hailed as a saint by some newspapers. Some of the hyperbole may have gone too far, but most of the praise was clearly deserved.

Bob Geldof has always insisted that 'halos get pretty heavy, and they rust quickly', but no other individual has had such a sustained impact on the world's conscience in recent times. His achievement in concentrating attention on the Central African famine has seen him nominated for the 1986 Nobel Peace Prize. . . .

During 1985 this 6ft 3in tall, thin singer did much to make the famine in Africa a cause which no government, or civilised man or woman, could ignore. He has ensured that many of the hungry have been fed and villages built, irrigation wells drilled, medical aid delivered – and the efforts of some relief agencies questioned. The Live Aid concerts have in turn been followed by similar events, including Fashion Aid in London and Sport Aid.

Geldof has steadfastly refused to take a salary from the organisation he has created. He confesses to being 'flat broke', but says simply, 'I've told everyone that every penny goes to Africa, so it's a matter of trust'.

He has told African leaders that he does not want 'any more boring speeches', and has also remarked to EEC administrators that he is 'fed up with red tape'. Everywhere his message has remained the same. 'We've kept millions alive, now we must give them a life – and that needs money.' If he had been a more sophisticated man, more conscious of the difficulties of political initiative in a complex world, Geldof might never have broken through the bureaucracies which too often ensnare international relief. But his impulsive candour, exuberance and Irish charm has seen him win every argument so far.

Check your understanding

1 Look at the text again. What do you think the following mean?

on the slide	(line 2)
single	(line 7)
flat broke	(line 34)
fed up	(line 39)

2 Find two words meaning 'help'.

3 Are the following sentences true or false according to the text?

a The popularity of the Boomtown Rats was growing.

b Everyone said that *Do They Know It's Christmas?* would have record sales.

c Bob Geldof was nominated for a humanitarian award in 1986.

d The rock musician brought food to many people.

e The Live Aid concert made Geldof a rich man.

Points for discussion

- Did your country show the Live Aid TV concert in 1985? What was the reaction to the purpose behind the event?
- There is famine because the world's population is growing and not enough food can be produced to feed everyone. Do you agree?
- Why might a more sophisticated man have failed to break through the bureaucracies?
- Why not simply give the surplus food in the West to the starving Africans? Could the Africans use up the European butter and grain surpluses?
- Which of the following do you think are best able to solve the problems of world famine?

farmers	actors
politicians	bureaucrats
rock singers	soldiers

- Harvests also fail in the USSR, the USA and Europe but this does not result in famine. Why not?
- Could you use your charm to win an argument?

Listening

Bob Geldof was interviewed recently about his latest money-raising project, 'Run For Your Life'. While you listen, make notes, then answer the questions below.

1 How much did Geldof originally aim to raise?

2 What was the amount actually collected?

3 Name three Aid programmes Geldof has organised.

4 Explain 'I thought that you could go to the well once too often . . .'

5 What event immediately follows the 'Race Against Time'?

6 Name some of the cities on the route of the 'Race Against Time'.

7 What prize was offered to two participants in the 'Run for Your Life' event?

8 State the main aim of Geldof's fund-raising activities.

GRAMMAR GUIDE

Conditional 3

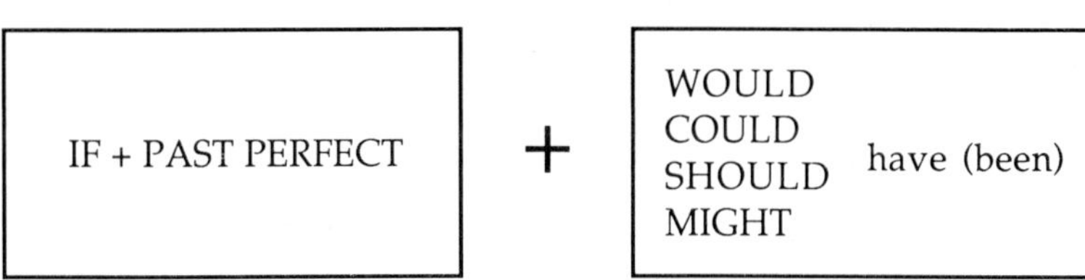
IF + PAST PERFECT + WOULD / COULD / SHOULD / MIGHT have (been)

This type of conditional refers to the past and is hypothetical and also impossible (because we cannot change the past!)
eg If he hadn't driven so fast he would not have had an accident.

Practice

1 Turn the statements below into Conditional 3 sentences, as in the example.

eg Bob Geldof made an effort to raise money and was able to help thousands of starving people.
If Bob Geldof *hadn't made* an effort to raise money, he *wouldn't have been able* to help thousands of starving people.

1. They took an early holiday on the South Coast and so they had beautiful weather.
2. Geldof wrote a song to raise money to help famine victims.
3. We left home late and got caught up in the Bank Holiday traffic jam.
4. She cheated in the exams but she was caught and disqualified.
5. We had dinner at our local Tandoori restaurant and both of us felt quite ill the next day.
6. I didn't listen to her directions on how to get to the club, and so I got hopelessly lost.

The Past Perfect can be inverted in Conditional 3 sentences for added emphasis.

eg If I had known you were coming, I'd have waited for you.
⇒ Had I known you were coming I'd have waited for you.
If they hadn't gone out for the evening, their house wouldn't have been burgled.
⇒ Had they not gone out for the evening, their house wouldn't have been burgled.

2 Rewrite the following sentences in two ways, first as Conditional 3 sentences with *if*, then with the Past Perfect inversion.

a They had no idea that their family would be large. They built a house that was too small.
b I lent him my car. I didn't know he had no driving licence.
c We worked hard for a year so that we could take a trip around the world.
d He passed all the exams with very high marks because he studied a lot.
e We didn't realise they were so tired, or we'd have taken them home.
f He didn't know we were all in the waiting room. He left the building.

3 Now make up five Conditional 3 sentences with the Past Perfect inversion about yourself, your friends or your family.
You might like to think about these:

a if you had lived somewhere else
b if you had been born in another town/country
c if you'd gone to a different school
d if you'd had different friends/met different people . . .

Vocabulary practice

Fill in the blanks in each of the following sentences, using the words in brackets.

1 Many societies are concerned with the ________ of cruelty to animals.
(*protection provision prevention projection*)

2 Bob Geldof appealed to the ________ of the world.
(*conscientiousness consciousness conscience consent*)

3 All the money will go to the ________ of famine relief.
(*course cause prevention ending*)

4 Banks and post offices were used to help in the ________ of money.
(*collation collocation compilation collection*)

5 Millions of people made ________ by credit card.
(*donors collections statements donations*)

Writing

Drawing on information contained in the reading text and listening passage, plus anything else you may know, write a profile of Bob Geldof. This can be as subjective or objective as you wish. It should be done with teenage readers in mind (it could be an article for a teen-magazine) and should not be more than 400 words.

DIARY pp. 78–81

Day(s) Date(s) Month Year

Texts

OK

Look at again

Ask the teacher

Look up in reference books

To remember

New Words

Grammar

Useful phrases